Microsoft®
Windows® 2000
Brief Edition

INTERACTIVE COMPUTING
SERIES

Kenneth C. Laudon
Kenneth Rosenblatt

Azimuth Interactive, Inc.

InformationTechnology

Irwin
McGraw-Hill

Boston   Burr Ridge, IL   Dubuque, IA   Madison, WI   New York   San Francisco   St. Louis
Bangkok   Bogotá   Caracas   Lisbon   London   Madrid   Mexico City   Milan   New Delhi   Seoul
Singapore   Sydney   Taipei   Toronto

McGraw-Hill Higher Education

*A Division of The **McGraw-Hill** Companies*

MICROSOFT WINDOWS 2000 BRIEF EDITION
Copyright © 2000 by The McGraw-Hill Companies, Inc. All rights reserved. Printed in the United States of America. Except as permitted under the United States Copyright Act of 1976, no part of this publication may be reproduced or distributed in any form or by any means, or stored in a data base or retrieval system, without the prior written permission of the publisher.

 This book is printed on recycled, acid-free paper containing 10% postconsumer waste.

1 2 3 4 5 6 7 8 9 0 QPD/QPD 9 0 9 8 7 6 5 4 3 2 1 0 9

ISBN   0-07-239964-3

Publisher: *David Kendric Brake*
Sponsoring editor: *Jodi McPherson*
Associate editor: *Steve Schuetz*
Developmental editors: *Erin Riley and Melissa Forte*
Senior marketing manager: *Jeff Parr*
Project manager: *Pat Frederickson*
Production supervisor: *Michael R. McCormick*
Freelance design coordinator: *Pam Verros*
Cover illustration: *Kip Henrie*
Supplement coordinator: *Marc Mattson*
Compositor: *Azimuth Interactive, Inc.*
Typeface: *10/12 Sabon*
Printer: *Quebecor Printing Book Group/Dubuque*

Library of Congress Catalog Card Number: 00-104683

http://www.mhhe.com

Microsoft® Windows® 2000
Brief Edition

INTERACTIVE COMPUTING SERIES

Kenneth C. Laudon
Kenneth Rosenblatt

Azimuth Interactive, Inc.

InformationTechnology

At **McGraw-Hill Higher Education**, we publish instructional materials targeted at the higher education market. In an effort to expand the tools of higher learning, we publish texts, lab manuals, study guides, testing materials, software, and multimedia products.

At **Irwin/McGraw-Hill** (a division of McGraw-Hill Higher Education), we realize technology will continue to create new mediums for professors and students to manage resources and communicate information with one another. We strive to provide the most flexible and complete teaching and learning tools available and offer solutions to the changing world of teaching and learning.

Irwin/McGraw-Hill is dedicated to providing the tools necessary for today's instructors and students to navigate the world of Information Technology successfully.

Seminar Series - Irwin/McGraw-Hill's Technology Connection seminar series offered across the country every year, demonstrates the latest technology products and encourages collaboration among teaching professionals.

Osborne/McGraw-Hill - A division of the McGraw-Hill Companies known for its best-selling Internet titles *Harley Hahn's Internet & Web Yellow Pages* and the *Internet Complete Reference*, offers an additional resource for certification and has strategic publishing relationships with corporations such as Corel Corporation and America Online. For more information, visit Osborne at www.osborne.com.

Digital Solutions - Irwin/McGraw-Hill is committed to publishing Digital Solutions. Taking your course online doesn't have to be a solitary venture. Nor does it have to be a difficult one. We offer several solutions, which will let you enjoy all the benefits of having course material online. For more information, visit www.mhhe.com/solutions/index.mhtml.

Packaging Options - For more about our discount options, contact your local Irwin/McGraw-Hill Sales representative at 1-800-338-3987, or visit our Web site at www.mhhe.com/it.

Interactive Computing Series

Goals/Philosophy
The *Interactive Computing Series* provides you with an illustrated interactive environment for learning software skills using Microsoft Office. The Interactive Computing Series is composed of both text and multimedia interactive CD-ROMs. The text and the CD-ROMs are closely coordinated. *It's up to you. You can choose how you want to learn.*

Approach
The *Interactive Computing Series* is the visual interactive way to develop and apply software skills. This skills-based approach coupled with its highly visual, two-page spread design allows the student to focus on a single skill without having to turn the page. A running case study is provided through the text, reinforcing the skills and giving a real-world focus to the learning process.

About the Book

The **Interactive Computing Series** offers *two levels* of instruction. Each level builds upon the previous level.

Brief lab manual - covers the basics of the application, contains two to four chapters.
Introductory lab manual - includes the material in the Brief textbook plus two to four additional chapters.

Each lesson is organized around **Skills**, **Concepts**, and **Steps (Do It!)**.

Each lesson is divided into a number of Skills. Each **Skill** is first explained at the top of the page.
Each **Concept** is a concise description of why the skill is useful and where it is commonly used.
Each **Step (Do It!)** contains the instructions on how to complete the skill.

About the CD-ROM

The CD-ROM provides a unique interactive environment for students where they learn to use software faster and remember it better. The CD-ROM is organized in a similar approach as the text: The **Skill** is defined, the **Concept** is explained in rich multimedia, and the student performs **Steps (Do It!)** within sections called Interactivities. There are at least <u>45 Interactivities per CD-ROM</u>. Some of the features of the CD-ROM are:

Simulated Environment - The Interactive Computing CD-ROM places students in a simulated controlled environment where they can practice and perform the skills of the application software.
Interactive Exercises - The student is asked to demonstrate command of a specific software skill. The student's actions are followed by a digital "TeacherWizard" that provides feedback.
SmartQuizzes - Provide performance-based assessment of the student at the end of each lesson.

Using the Book

In the book, each skill is described in a two-page graphical spread (Figure 1). The left side of the two-page spread describes the skill, the concept, and the steps needed to perform the skill. The right side of the spread uses screen shots to show you how the screen should look at key stages.

Figure 1

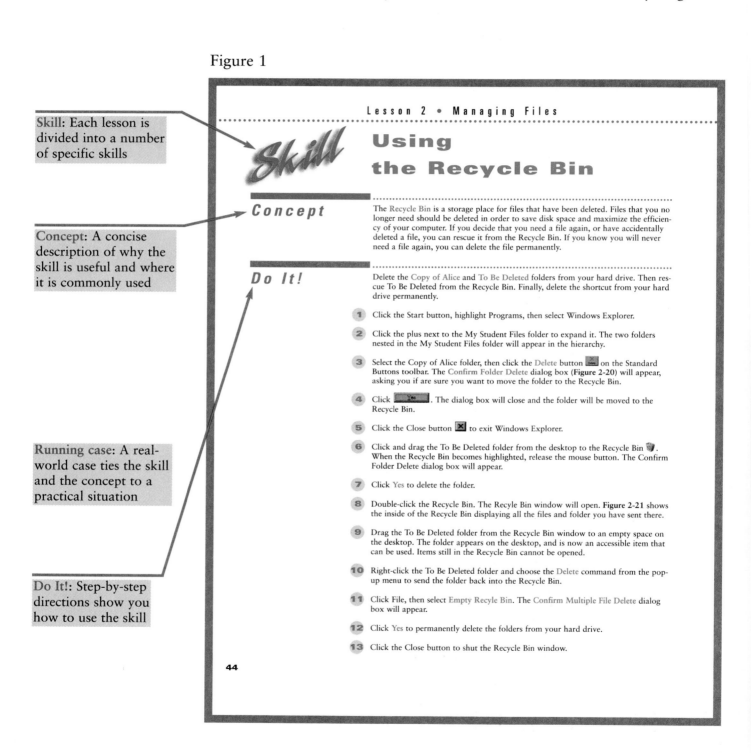

Skill: Each lesson is divided into a number of specific skills

Concept: A concise description of why the skill is useful and where it is commonly used

Running case: A real-world case ties the skill and the concept to a practical situation

Do It!: Step-by-step directions show you how to use the skill

Lesson 2 • Managing Files

Skill

Using the Recycle Bin

Concept

The Recycle Bin is a storage place for files that have been deleted. Files that you no longer need should be deleted in order to save disk space and maximize the efficiency of your computer. If you decide that you need a file again, or have accidentally deleted a file, you can rescue it from the Recycle Bin. If you know you will never need a file again, you can delete the file permanently.

Do It!

Delete the Copy of Alice and To Be Deleted folders from your hard drive. Then rescue To Be Deleted from the Recycle Bin. Finally, delete the shortcut from your hard drive permanently.

1. Click the Start button, highlight Programs, then select Windows Explorer.

2. Click the plus next to the My Student Files folder to expand it. The two folders nested in the My Student Files folder will appear in the hierarchy.

3. Select the Copy of Alice folder, then click the Delete button on the Standard Buttons toolbar. The Confirm Folder Delete dialog box (**Figure 2-20**) will appear, asking you if you are sure you want to move the folder to the Recycle Bin.

4. Click Yes. The dialog box will close and the folder will be moved to the Recycle Bin.

5. Click the Close button to exit Windows Explorer.

6. Click and drag the To Be Deleted folder from the desktop to the Recycle Bin. When the Recycle Bin becomes highlighted, release the mouse button. The Confirm Folder Delete dialog box will appear.

7. Click Yes to delete the folder.

8. Double-click the Recycle Bin. The Recyle Bin window will open. **Figure 2-21** shows the inside of the Recycle Bin displaying all the files and folder you have sent there.

9. Drag the To Be Deleted folder from the Recycle Bin window to an empty space on the desktop. The folder appears on the desktop, and is now an accessible item that can be used. Items still in the Recycle Bin cannot be opened.

10. Right-click the To Be Deleted folder and choose the Delete command from the pop-up menu to send the folder back into the Recycle Bin.

11. Click File, then select Empty Recycle Bin. The Confirm Multiple File Delete dialog box will appear.

12. Click Yes to permanently delete the folders from your hard drive.

13. Click the Close button to shut the Recycle Bin window.

44

End-of-Lesson Features

In the book, the learning in each lesson is reinforced at the end by a quiz and a skills review called Interactivity, which provides step-by-step exercises and real-world problems for the students to solve independently.

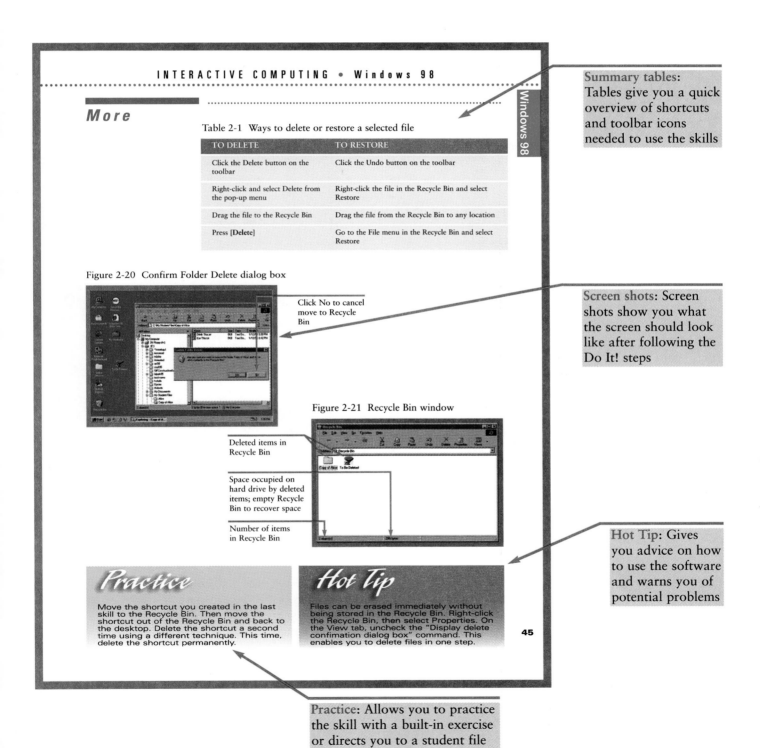

INTERACTIVE COMPUTING • Windows 98

Windows 98

More

Summary tables: Tables give you a quick overview of shortcuts and toolbar icons needed to use the skills

Table 2-1 Ways to delete or restore a selected file

TO DELETE	TO RESTORE
Click the Delete button on the toolbar	Click the Undo button on the toolbar
Right-click and select Delete from the pop-up menu	Right-click the file in the Recycle Bin and select Restore
Drag the file to the Recycle Bin	Drag the file from the Recycle Bin to any location
Press [Delete]	Go to the File menu in the Recycle Bin and select Restore

Figure 2-20 Confirm Folder Delete dialog box

Click No to cancel move to Recycle Bin

Screen shots: Screen shots show you what the screen should look like after following the Do It! steps

Figure 2-21 Recycle Bin window

Deleted items in Recycle Bin

Space occupied on hard drive by deleted items; empty Recycle Bin to recover space

Number of items in Recycle Bin

Hot Tip: Gives you advice on how to use the software and warns you of potential problems

Practice

Move the shortcut you created in the last skill to the Recycle Bin. Then move the shortcut out of the Recycle Bin and back to the desktop. Delete the shortcut a second time using a different technique. This time, delete the shortcut permanently.

Hot Tip

Files can be erased immediately without being stored in the Recycle Bin. Right-click the Recycle Bin, then select Properties. On the View tab, uncheck the "Display delete confimation dialog box" command. This enables you to delete files in one step.

45

Practice: Allows you to practice the skill with a built-in exercise or directs you to a student file

Using the Interactive CD-ROM

The Interactive Computing multimedia CD-ROM provides an unparalleled learning environment in which you can learn software skills faster and better than in books alone. The CD-ROM creates a unique interactive environment in which you can learn to use software faster and remember it better. The CD-ROM uses the same lessons, skills, concepts, and Do It! steps as found in the book, but presents the material using voice, video, animation, and precise simulation of the software you are learning. A typical CD-ROM contents screen shows the major elements of a lesson (see Figure 2 below).

Skills list: A list of skills allows you to jump directly to any skill you want to learn or review, including interactive sessions with the TeacherWizard

Figure 2

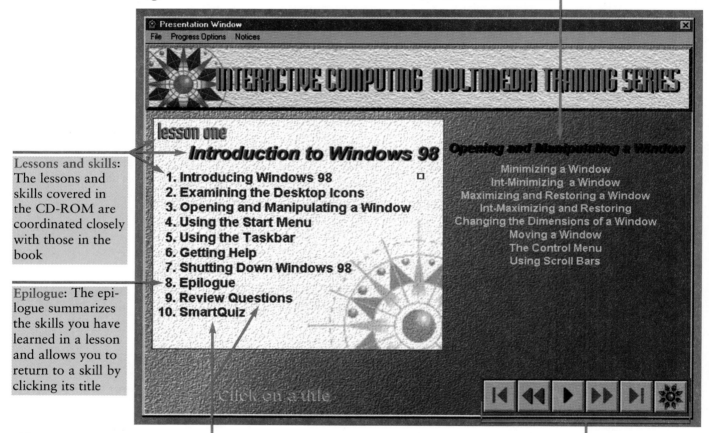

Lessons and skills: The lessons and skills covered in the CD-ROM are coordinated closely with those in the book

Epilogue: The epilogue summarizes the skills you have learned in a lesson and allows you to return to a skill by clicking its title

Review Questions and SmartQuiz: Review Questions test your knowledge of the concepts covered in the lesson; SmartQuiz tests your ability to accomplish tasks in a simulated software environment

User controls: Precise and simple user controls permit you to start, stop, pause, jump forward or backward one sentence, or jump forward or backward an entire skill. A single navigation star takes you back to the lesson's table of contents

Unique Features of the CD-ROM: TeacherWizard™ and SmartQuiz™

Interactive Computing: Software Skills offers many leading-edge features on the CD-ROM currently found in no other learning product on the market. One such feature is *interactive exercises* in which you are asked to demonstrate your command of a software skill in a precisely simulated software environment. Your actions are followed closely by a digital TeacherWizard that guides you with additional information if you make a mistake. When you complete the action called for by the TeacherWizard correctly, you are congratulated and prompted to continue the lesson. If you make a mistake, the TeacherWizard gently lets you know: "No, that's not the right icon. Click on the Folder icon on the left side of the top toolbar to open a file." No matter how many mistakes you make, the TeacherWizard is there to help you.

Another leading-edge feature is the end-of-lesson SmartQuiz. Unlike the multiple choice and matching questions found in the book quiz, the SmartQuiz puts you in a simulated digital software world and asks you to show your mastery of skills while actually working with the software (Figure 3).

Figure 3

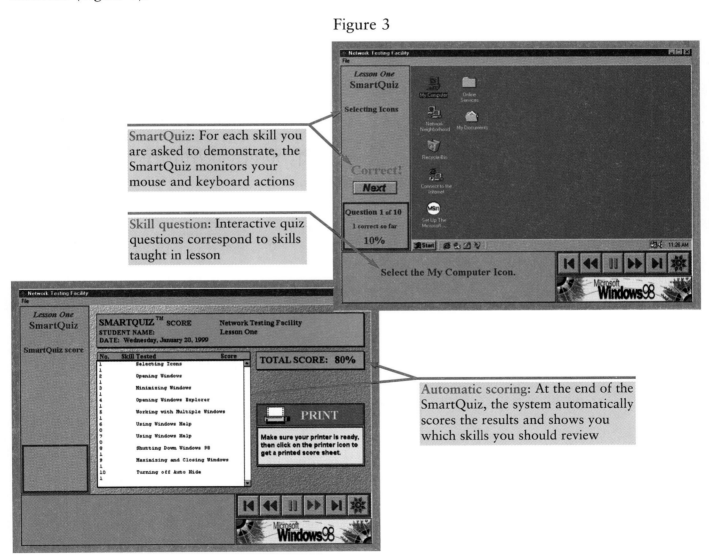

SmartQuiz: For each skill you are asked to demonstrate, the SmartQuiz monitors your mouse and keyboard actions

Skill question: Interactive quiz questions correspond to skills taught in lesson

Automatic scoring: At the end of the SmartQuiz, the system automatically scores the results and shows you which skills you should review

Teaching Resources

The following is a list of supplemental material available with the Interactive Computing Series:

Skills Assessment
Irwin/McGraw-Hill offers two innovative systems, ATLAS and SimNet, which take testing beyond the basics with pre- and post-assessment capabilities.
ATLAS (Active Testing and Learning Assessment Software) – available for the *Interactive Computing Series* – is our live-in-the-application Skills Assessment tool. ATLAS allows students to perform tasks while working live within the Office applications environment. ATLAS is web-enabled and customizable to meet the needs of your course. ATLAS is available for Office 2000.
SimNet (Simulated Network Assessment Product) – available for the *Interactive Computing Series* – permits you to test the actual software skills students learn about the Microsoft Office applications in a simulated environment. SimNet is web-enabled and is available for Office 97 and Office 2000.

Instructor's Resource Kits
The Instructor's Resource Kit provides professors with all of the ancillary material needed to teach a course. Irwin/McGraw-Hill is dedicated to providing instructors with the most effective instruction resources available. Many of these resources are available at our Information Technology Supersite www.mhhe.com/it. Our Instructor's Kits are available on CD-ROM and contain the following:

>Diploma by Brownstone - is the most flexible, powerful, and easy-to-use computerized testing system available in higher education. The diploma system allows professors to create an Exam as a printed version, as a LAN-based Online version, and as an Internet version. Diploma includes grade book features, which automate the entire testing process.
>Instructor's Manual - Includes:
>-Solutions to all lessons and end-of-unit material
>-Teaching Tips
>-Teaching Strategies
>-Additional exercises
>PowerPoint Slides - NEW to the Interactive Computing Series, all of the figures from the application textbooks are available in PowerPoint slides for presentation purposes.
>Student Data Files - To use the Interactive Computing Series, students must have Student Data Files to complete practice and test sessions. The instructor and students using this text in classes are granted the right to post the student files on any network or stand-alone computer, or to distribute the files on individual diskettes. The student files may be downloaded from our IT Supersite at www.mhhe.com/it.
>Series Web Site - Available at www.mhhe.com/cit/apps/laudon.

Digital Solutions
>Pageout Lite - is designed if you're just beginning to explore Web site options. Pageout Lite is great for posting your own material online. You may choose one of three templates, type in your material, and Pageout Lite instantly converts it to HTML.
>Pageout - is our Course Web site Development Center. Pageout offers a Syllabus page, Web site address, Online Learning Center Content, online exercises and quizzes, gradebook, discussion board, an area for students to build their own Web pages, and all the features of Pageout Lite. For more information please visit the Pageout Web site at www.mhla.net/pageout.

Teaching Resources (continued)

OLC/Series Web Sites - Online Learning Centers (OLCs)/Series Sites are accessible through our Supersite at www.mhhe.com/it. Our Online Learning Centers/Series Sites provide pedagogical features and supplements for our titles online. Students can point and click their way to key terms, learning objectives, chapter overviews, PowerPoint slides, exercises, and Web links.

The McGraw-Hill Learning Architecture (MHLA) - is a complete course delivery system. MHLA gives professors ownership in the way digital content is presented to the class through online quizzing, student collaboration, course administration, and content management. For a walk-through of MHLA visit the MHLA Web site at www.mhla.net.

Packaging Options - For more about our discount options, contact your local Irwin/McGraw-Hill Sales representative at 1-800-338-3987 or visit our Web site at www.mhhe.com/it.

Visit www.mhhe.com/it
THE ONLY SITE WITH ALL YOUR CIT AND MIS NEEDS.

Acknowledgments

The Interactive Computing Series is a cooperative effort of many individuals, each contributing to an overall team effort. The Interactive Computing team is composed of instructional designers, writers, multimedia designers, graphic artists, and programmers. Our goal is to provide you and your instructor with the most powerful and enjoyable learning environment using both traditional text and new interactive multimedia techniques. Interactive Computing is tested rigorously in both CD-ROM and text formats prior to publication.

Our special thanks to Trisha O'Shea, our Editor for computer applications and concepts, and to Jodi McPherson, Marketing Director for Computer Information Systems. Both Trisha and Jodi have provided exceptional market awareness and understanding, along with enthusiasm and support for the project. They have inspired us all to work closely together. Steven Schuetz provided valuable technical review of our interactive versions, and Charles Pelto contributed superb quality assurance. Thanks to our Publisher, David Brake, and Mike Junior, Vice-President and Editor-in-Chief. They have given us tremendous encouragement and the needed support to tackle seemingly impossible projects.

The Azimuth team members who contributed to the textbooks and CD-ROM multimedia program are:

Ken Rosenblatt (Textbooks Project Manager and Writer)
Russell Polo (Chief Programmer)
Steven D. Pileggi (Multimedia Project Director)
Jason Eiseman (Technical Writer)
Michael W. Domis (Technical Writer)
Robin Pickering (Developmental Editor, Quality Assurance)
Stefon Westry (Multimedia Designer)
Caroline Kasterine (Multimedia Designer, Writer)
Joseph S. Gina (Multimedia Designer)
Irene Pileggi (Multimedia Designer, Writer)
Josie Torlish (Quality Assurance)
Dan Langan (Multimedia Designer)

Contents

Windows 2000 Brief Edition

Contents

Continued

L E S S O N

1

INTRODUCTION TO WINDOWS 2000

Windows 2000 is an **operating system** that controls the basic functions of your computer, such as loading and running programs, saving data, and displaying information on the screen. Operating system software is different from application software, such as a word processor or spreadsheet program, which you apply to letter writing or calculating data. Instead, operating system software provides the **user interface** — the visual display on the screen that you use to operate the computer by choosing which programs to run and how to organize your work. Windows 2000 offers a **graphical user interface** or **GUI** (pronounced "gooey") that presents you with pictorial representations of computer functions and data.

It is through these pictures, or icons, that you interact with the computer. **Data files** are represented by icons that look like pieces of paper, and can be organized into groups called **folders**, which look like manila folders. The **My Computer** icon, represented by a small desktop PC, allows you to organize these files and folders. Other icons allow you to run programs such as a word processor, a Web browser, or Windows' built-in file manager, **Windows Explorer.**

Windows 2000 is a powerful operating system that allows you to perform a variety of high-level tasks. Windows 2000 is actually the successor to the Windows NT 4.0 operating system, but it looks, acts, and responds in much the same manner as Windows 98. For instance, the GUI is very similar, using many of the same icons as Windows 98. It also includes integrated Web features. Thus, Windows 2000 gives you the ease of use of Windows 98, with the power, stability, and security previously provided by Windows NT. This makes Windows 2000 an ideal tool for operating a business whether it is run on a laptop computer, a desktop system, or a large business server.

Windows 2000 is easy to use and can be customized with the preferences and options that you desire. Built-in programs called **Accessories** can be used to help you with day-to-day tasks. **Help** offers fast tutorial and troubleshooting advice. This book will teach you about the basic elements of Windows 2000 and how to use them. You will learn file management, advanced Windows functions, Internet skills, and some of the other special features of Windows 2000.

Examining the Desktop Icons

Concept

The screen you see when Windows 2000 completes the StartUp procedure is called the desktop. Do not be surprised if your desktop does not look exactly like the one pictured in **Figure 1-1** as computer setups vary from machine to machine. (Throughout this book the appearance of your desktop and windows will depend on the software installed and the configuration of various settings of your computer.) Like the desk that you are sitting at, the Windows desktop is the workspace on which all actions are performed. On the left side of your screen you will see small pictures called icons. Icons are pictorial representations of a task, program, folder, or file. Each icon represents an application or utility that you can start. You use the mouse — a hand-controlled input device that, when connected to the computer and moved along a clean, flat surface, will move the graphical pointer around the screen — to double-click an icon to open an application or a file. The buttons on the mouse are used to give commands, and there are four basic ways you can use the mouse: pointing, clicking, double-clicking, and dragging.

Do It!

Use the mouse to move the pointer ⇖ around the desktop to explore the desktop icons.

1. Using the mouse, move the pointer over various areas of the desktop to get a feel for how the pointer moves in relation to the motion of the mouse. Positioning the pointer over an item is called pointing.

2. Locate the My Computer icon on the desktop; it resembles a desktop PC. Place the pointer on the icon and click the left mouse button once. This will highlight the icon, indicating that it has been selected. Click a blank area of the screen to undo this selection. Note that primary mouse functions are done using the left button.

3. Double-clicking is done to open a program, file, or window. Open the My Computer window by placing the pointer on the My Computer icon and clicking the left mouse button twice quickly. The My Computer window, shown in **Figure 1-2**, will appear on the desktop.

4. To close the window you have just opened, position the pointer over the Close button ☒ in the upper-right corner and click the left mouse button.

5. Icons are not fixed on the desktop and can be moved by dragging. Move the pointer to the My Computer icon, then click and hold down the button. You have grabbed the icon.

6. With the mouse button held down, move the icon by dragging it to the center of your desktop. A faint image of the icon will appear to indicate the current position of the icon on the desktop. Let go of the mouse button to drop the icon into position. Then return the icon to its original position.

More

Windows 2000 allows you to change the way you work with icons so that the interface behaves more like a Web page. To make this change, click on the word Tools on the Menu bar in the My Computer window. This will cause a list of commands, called a menu, to appear. Click the Folder Options command on the Tools menu to open the Folder Options dialog box. Whenever you see an ellipsis (three dots) following a command, it indicates that the command will open a dialog box revealing options for the execution of the command. The dialog box will open to a tab named General. In the bottom section of this dialog box, the default option is Double-click to open an item (single-click to select). This is the traditional way of interacting with Windows icons. If you select the first option in the section, Single-click to open an item (point to select), the operating system will switch to a Web-like environment where pointing and clicking are concerned.

Figure 1-1 The Windows desktop

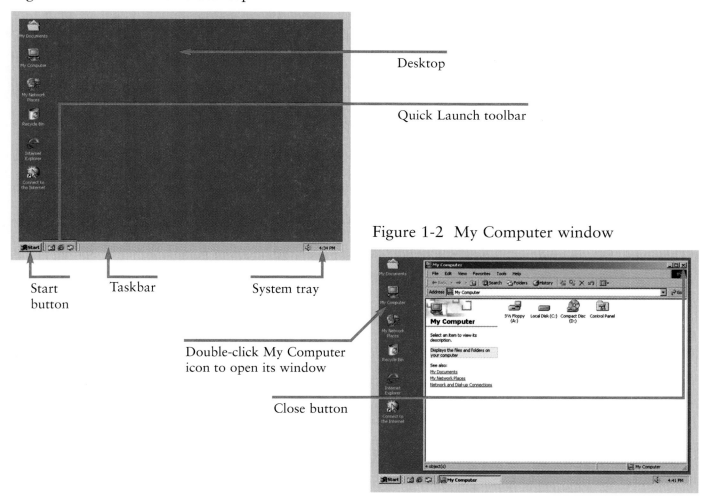

Desktop

Quick Launch toolbar

Start button

Taskbar

System tray

Figure 1-2 My Computer window

Double-click My Computer icon to open its window

Close button

Practice

Open the My Documents window by double-clicking its icon. Use the Close button to close the window.

Hot Tip

If your mouse movements are running off the mouse pad, position the mouse pointer in the middle of the screen, and then pick up the mouse and place it in the middle of the mouse pad.

Opening, Moving, and Resizing a Window

Concept

As you saw in the previous Skill, icons are pictorial representations of different items on your computer, the most common of which are folders, files, and applications. When you double-click an icon to open it, its contents are revealed in a window or on-screen frame. It is in this window that you interact with a program or utility. Windows are flexible and can be moved, resized, reshaped, and even hidden.

Do It!

Open the My Computer window, then resize, move, minimize, and close it.

1. Double-click the My Computer icon. The My Computer window will open, as shown in **Figure 1-3**.

2. You cannot resize or move a window that is maximized or fills the entire desktop. Look at the three sizing buttons at the right end of the window's title bar, the band at the top of the window that contains the name of the application. The middle button's appearance will change depending on the window's state. If the Restore button ▣ is visible, click it so the window will no longer be maximized. Once the window is restored to its previous size the button will change to the Maximize button ▢.

3. Position the mouse pointer on the right edge of the window. This will change the pointer to a double arrow ↔ that is used to resize an object. In Windows 2000, the appearance of the mouse pointer changes to reflect its function during various tasks.

4. Click and hold the left mouse button, drag the edge of the window towards the center of the screen, and then let go of the mouse button to drop the side of the window into place. As you drag the mouse, the border of the window will move with the double arrow, toolbar buttons will disappear (don't worry their respective commands can still be accessed through menus), and scroll bars (see More below) may appear. This action may be repeated on any of the window's four sides or at any corner. Resizing from the corner will alter both the height and width of the window.

5. Windows can be dragged and dropped just as icons can. Move the pointer over the title bar of the My Computer window, and then click and hold the left mouse button to grab the window.

6. With the mouse button depressed, drag the window to another area of the desktop.

Figure 1-3 Components of a window

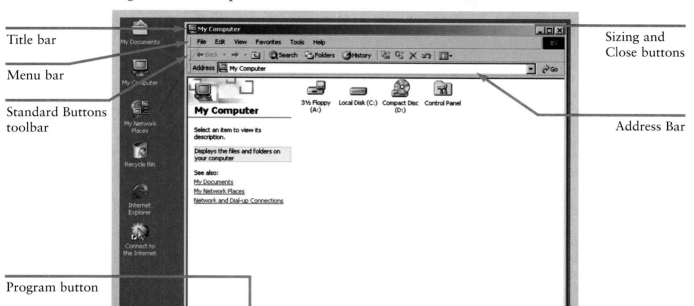

Title bar

Menu bar

Standard Buttons toolbar

Program button

Sizing and Close buttons

Address Bar

Status Bar

Table 1-1 Sizing buttons

SIZING BUTTON		USE
Maximize	▣	Enlarges the window so that it fills the entire screen, with the taskbar remaining visible
Restore	▣	Returns the window to its previous size
Minimize	▬	Shrinks the window so it only appears as a program button on the taskbar
Close	✕	Closes a window or program

Opening, Moving, and Resizing (continued)

Do It!

7 Click the Minimize button ▬. The My Computer window will disappear from the desktop and be reduced to a program button on the taskbar, as shown in **Figure 1-4**.

8 Click the My Computer program button to restore the window to its previous size.

9 Click File on the menu bar. The File menu will appear as shown in **Figure 1-5**.

10 Position the pointer over the last command, Close, to highlight it, and then click the mouse button. The Close command will be executed, just as it would if you clicked the Close button ☒, and the window will disappear from the desktop.

More

When a window is too small to display all of its information, scroll bars (**Figure 1-6**) will appear on the right and/or bottom edges of the window. Scroll bars are context-sensitive objects and only appear when the situation is appropriate. The scroll bars are used to slide information inside the window so you can see additional contents of the window. If you need to scroll slowly, or only a short distance, click a scroll bar arrow located at the end of the scroll bar. The scroll bar box indicates where you are located in the window. Clicking above or below the scroll bar box moves the display in large increments. Dragging the scroll bar box allows you to control the slide of the window's information precisely.

In the above Skill you clicked the My Computer program button to unhide the window and make it active. An active window is identified by its highlighted title bar, and will be the frontmost window on your desktop if more than one program is running. You can also click the program button of a visible window to minimize it. Right-clicking a program button, clicking it with the right mouse button, will cause a pop-up menu to appear with commands that mirror those of the sizing buttons. These commands can also be found by clicking the Control icon, the icon at the left edge of the title bar representing the application, or by right-clicking the title bar. Right-clicking will usually cause a context-sensitive menu to appear. This menu will contain commands that relate to the task you are performing. Double-clicking the title bar will restore or maximize a window.

Figure 1-4 Minimized My Computer window

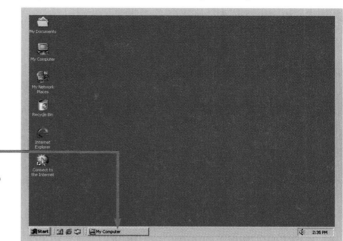

My Computer window minimized to a program button on the taskbar

Figure 1-5 Working with the File menu

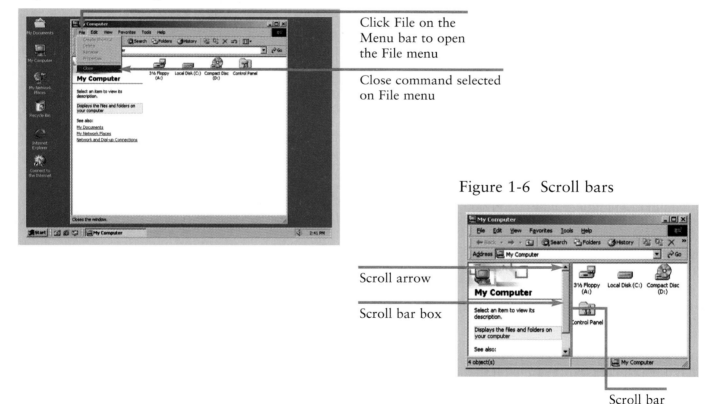

Click File on the Menu bar to open the File menu

Close command selected on File menu

Figure 1-6 Scroll bars

Scroll arrow

Scroll bar box

Scroll bar

Practice

Open and maximize the My Documents window. Then restore the window and drag its right border outward. Close the window when you are done.

Hot Tip

Clicking the Show Desktop button ▧ minimizes all open windows. Clicking the button again opens all of the previously visible windows.

Using the Start Menu

Concept

The Start button ![Start], located on the left side of the taskbar, provides a quick and easy way to open and organize the applications found on your computer. Clicking the Start button opens a special menu called the Start menu, shown expanded in **Figure 1-7**, that contains left-to-right lists of program groups. Items with an arrow ▶ next to them contain submenus. Pointing to an item highlights it; and a simple click will then open the program you wish to use.

Do It!

Use the Start button to access the Start menu and start Windows Explorer, a file management utility that will be discussed in detail in Lesson 2 (if you do not see an item that is named in this Skill, click the double arrow at the bottom of the menu).

1 Click the Start button ![Start] on the taskbar, usually located at the bottom of your desktop. The Start menu will open. Do not be surprised if your Start menu does not match **Figure 1-7** exactly. The appearance of your Start menu depends on the software installed and the shortcuts created on your computer.

2 Position the pointer over Programs (notice the little arrow) to bring up the Programs menu. The Programs menu contains a list of shortcuts to some of the applications found on your hard drive, as well as folders that hold groups of related shortcuts to other frequently used programs and utilities.

3 Guide the pointer to Accessories, which is likely located at the top of the Programs menu. The Accessories menu will appear alongside the Programs menu.

4 Move the mouse pointer over to the Accessories menu and click the program named Windows Explorer to launch it. **Figure 1-8** displays an open Windows Explorer, with the My Documents folder selected. Notice that a program button displaying the name of the folder selected in Windows Explorer has appeared on the taskbar.

5 Click the Close button ![X] on the title bar to exit Windows Explorer.

More

Items on the Start menu and its submenus are really shortcuts to the actual folders and files that they represent.

The Documents menu contains a list of the files that have been opened most recently so that you can access your most recently and most often used data quickly.

On the Settings menu you will find folders that contain utilities for altering your computer's software and hardware settings. The way you interact with your desktop, the folders on it, the taskbar, and printers can all be altered through icons on the Settings menu.

One of the keys to using a computer is being able to locate the data you need. The Search menu offers you multiple ways in which to find information. You can search for files or folders on your computer, content on the World Wide Web, and people in locally stored address books and Internet directories.

Figure 1-7 Start menu

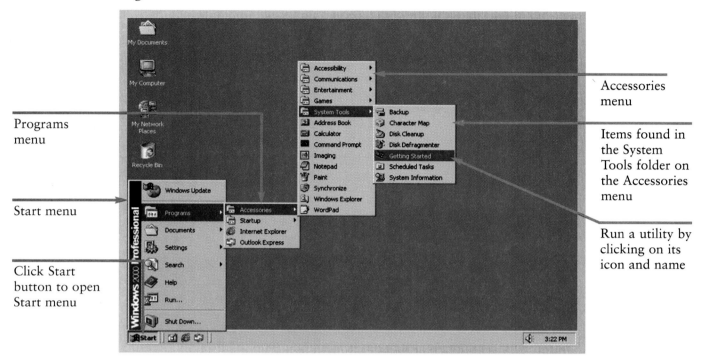

Accessories menu

Items found in the System Tools folder on the Accessories menu

Run a utility by clicking on its icon and name

Programs menu

Start menu

Click Start button to open Start menu

Figure 1-8 Windows Explorer

Practice

Use the Start button to open the Printers folder on the Settings menu. If your computer is hooked up to a printer or printers, the name(s) will appear in this window. Close the window from the title bar.

Hot Tip

The Start menu right-click pop-up menu has commands for quickly opening Windows Explorer and the Search feature.

 **Using the Taskbar**

Concept

The taskbar is your guide to the applications running on your system. Each open application creates its own program button on the taskbar, so switching between programs is as simple as the click of a button. While the taskbar is usually found at the bottom of the desktop, it is neither fixed in size nor location.

Do It!

Use the taskbar to open two applications and switch between them. Then, move and resize the taskbar.

1. Click the Start button to open the Start menu, highlight Programs, highlight Accessories, and then select Windows Explorer.

2. Click the Start button, highlight Programs, highlight Accessories, and then select Calculator. The calculator will open and two windows will be on your desktop with their respective program buttons on the taskbar, as shown in **Figure 1-9.**

3. Click the Windows Explorer program button, which is labeled My Documents. The Windows Explorer window will become active, moving to the foreground of the desktop. Notice that its title bar is now blue, and its program button is indented.

4. Click the Calculator button to make the Calculator window active.

5. Position the mouse pointer on the top edge of the taskbar. The pointer will change to a vertical double arrow when it is in the correct spot.

6. Press and hold the mouse button and drag the top of the taskbar up, until it is three times its original height. The taskbar can be enlarged to up to half of your desktop.

7. Click a blank space on the taskbar, and then hold the mouse button down while dragging the taskbar to the right edge of your desktop, as shown in **Figure 1-10.** The taskbar can be placed on the top, bottom, left, or right of the desktop.

8. Drag the taskbar back to its original place on the desktop and then resize it so it is one program button high.

9. Click each application's Close button to remove the windows from the desktop.

More

Additional taskbar settings can be found in the Taskbar Properties dialog box, accessed by highlighting Settings on the Start menu and then clicking the Taskbar & Start Menu command on the Settings menu. When you open this dialog box you will see five options on the General tab. Those with a check mark are turned on. The Always on top option prevents any window from obscuring the taskbar. With Auto hide turned on, the taskbar will drop out of sight when it is not in use. Move the pointer to the bottom of the desktop to make it reappear. The relative size of your Start menu items is controlled with the Show small icons in Start menu. You can turn the taskbar clock on or off with the Show Clock command. The Use Personalized Menus command permits Windows to hide the menu items that you do not use frequently. When you do need to access a hidden item, click on the double arrow at the bottom of the menu to expand it to its full size.

Figure 1-9 Two open applications

Inactive application
window

Active application
window

Active program
button

Inactive program
button

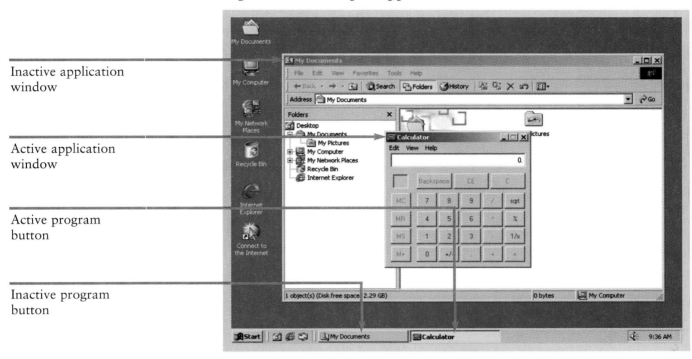

Figure 1-10 Resized and moved taskbar

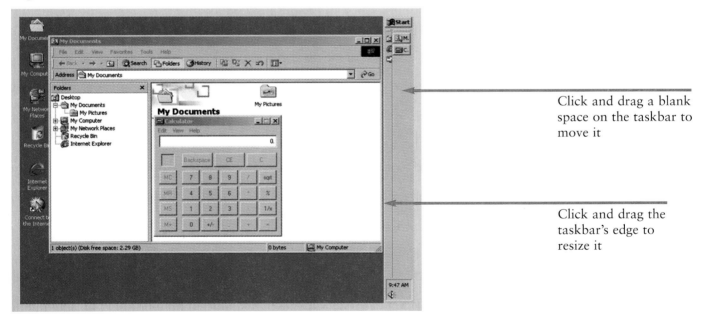

Click and drag a blank
space on the taskbar to
move it

Click and drag the
taskbar's edge to
resize it

Practice

Turn on the Auto hide taskbar option. Then open Windows Explorer, My Computer, and Calculator. Practice moving among the open windows. If you do not like the Auto hide option, turn it off again.

Hot Tip

You can move between open applications by holding [Alt] and then pressing [Tab]. Press [Tab] again to cycle through the list of all running applications. Release the [Alt] key when the correct icon is selected. Right-click the taskbar for more options.

Using Menus

Concept

A menu is a list of related operations, also known as commands, that you use to perform specific tasks. The menus that are available to you in any particular window are listed on the Menu bar, which is situated just below the window's title bar. Each Windows program has its own selection of menus, though many are similar. To access a menu, simply click on its menu title on the Menu bar. Some menu commands have shortcut buttons that allow you to execute them by clicking on a toolbar button. You will also find that many commands have keyboard shortcuts. If you prefer the keyboard to the mouse, Windows also provides a way to open all menus and choose any command without clicking.

Do It!

Examine and use a typical menu in the My Computer window.

1 Double-click the My Computer icon to open its window.

2 Click View on the Menu bar to open the View menu, shown in **Figure 1-11**.

3 You will notice that in addition to commands, several symbols appear on the menu. A right-pointing triangle after a command indicates that the command has a submenu. Point to the Toolbars command with the mouse to reveal the Toolbars submenu.

4 Move the mouse pointer down to the Status Bar command. The Toolbars submenu closes. The check mark to the left of the Status Bar command indicates that the feature is currently turned on. A bullet next to a command, tells you which command in a set is currently active. Only one command in a set such as the icon view commands may be active at a time.

5 Open the Toolbars submenu again. Then click the Standard Buttons command, which is turned on, to turn it off. The menu closes and the Standard Buttons toolbar disappears, as shown in **Figure 1-12**.

6 You can also use the keyboard to open a menu and execute a command. When you press the [Alt] key with the My Computer window active, one letter in each menu title is underlined. Pressing this letter will open the corresponding menu. Press [Alt], then press [V] to open the View menu.

7 Each command on a menu also has an underlined letter. Pressing this letter on the keyboard initiates the command. Press [T] to open the Toolbars submenu. Then Press [S] to execute the Standard Buttons command from the submenu, turning the Standard Buttons toolbar back on.

More

Some commands have keyboard shortcuts that you can use to avoid opening menus altogether. You can learn many of these shortcuts simply by seeing them listed on a menu. For example, if you open the Edit menu in the My Computer window, you will see that the Select All command is followed by [Ctrl]+[A]. This means that you can use the Select All command by holding down the [Ctrl] key and pressing [A].

Figure 1-11 View menu

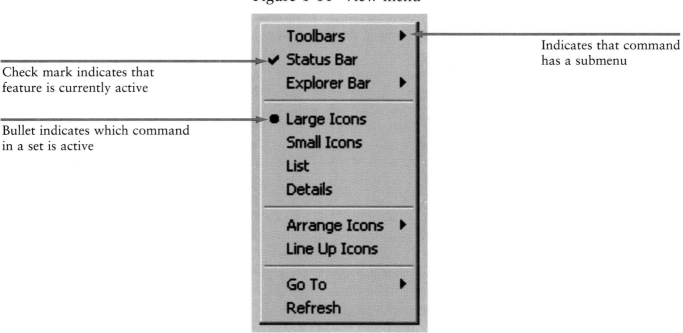

Check mark indicates that
feature is currently active

Bullet indicates which command
in a set is active

Indicates that command
has a submenu

Figure 1-12 My Computer window without Standard Buttons

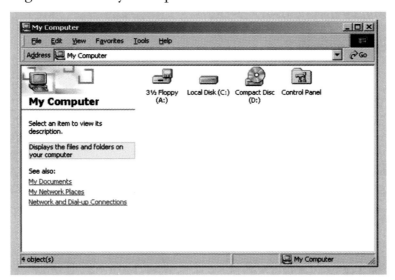

Practice

Open the My Computer window by double-clicking its icon. Then use the Close command on the File menu to close the window.

Hot Tip

Once a menu has been opened, you can use the arrow keys to move from command to command (up and down arrows) or from menu to menu (left and right arrows). Press [Enter] to execute a highlighted command.

Using Dialog Boxes

Concept

Some commands require additional information before Windows will perform the operations that accompany them. In these cases, a dialog box will appear. Dialog boxes allow you to customize a command's options according to your needs or preferences. Commands that include a dialog box are followed on a menu by three dots, called an ellipsis.

Do It!

Open the WordPad application, and then use the Print command to access and examine the Print dialog box.

1 Click **Start**, highlight Programs, then highlight Accessories, and then click WordPad. WordPad, Windows 2000's built-in word processor, will open.

2 To add text to a WordPad document, you can simply begin typing. Type Your Name's dialog box practice. Your document should look like **Figure 1-13**.

3 Open the File menu and click on the Print command. The Print dialog box will appear, as shown in **Figure 1-14**. The Print dialog box contains a number of common dialog box features, each connected to a specific printing option. Refer to the figure to gain an understanding of how each of these features works.

4 Click the Cancel button **Cancel** . The dialog box closes without executing the Print command.

5 Close the WordPad window. Windows will ask you if you want to save changes to the document. Click **No** .

More

Dialog boxes contain their own help tool. In the upper-right corner of a dialog box, you will find a button marked with a question mark. If you click on this button, a question mark will be attached to your mouse pointer. When you click on any dialog box feature with this pointer, a ScreenTip (**Figure 1-15**) will appear that explains the feature. Click the mouse button again to erase the ScreenTip and restore the pointer to its normal state.

Figure 1-15 Example of a dialog box ScreenTip

If you have selected more than one copy, specifies whether you want the copies to be collated.

Figure 1-13 WordPad document

Click Save button to save a WordPad document

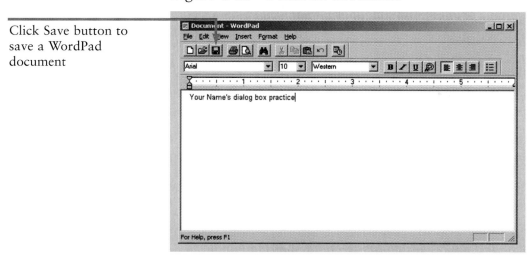

Figure 1-14 Dialog box features

Click tabs to access additional options

Click to get help on dialog box items

Click check box to activate associated option

Use text box to enter a value

Radio buttons allow you to select one option in a set

Click up or down arrow to change value in spin box

Click to execute command

Click to perform operation without closing dialog box

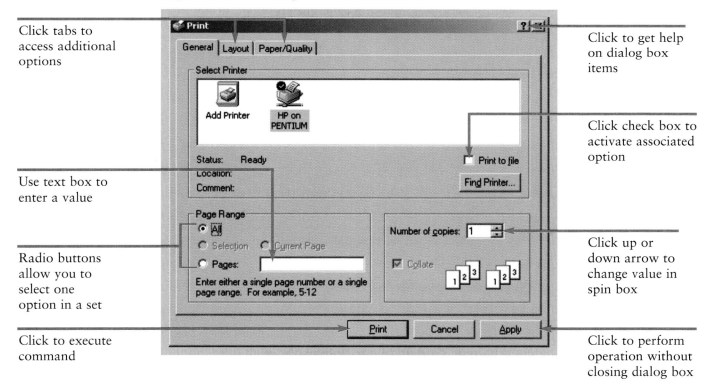

Practice

Find three other WordPad commands that use dialog boxes. View the features of each dialog box.

Hot Tip

When a dialog box has more than one option you can use the [Tab] key to cycle through the options.

Getting Help

Concept

You might find that you need a little assistance along the way as you explore Windows 2000. The Help files provide you with an extensive list of topics that provide aid, troubleshooting advice, and tips and tricks. You can use Help while you work, and even print topics when it is inconvenient to use Help on the fly.

Do It!

Use the Windows 2000 Help facility to learn about working with programs and word processing.

1 Click Start, then click Help on the Start menu. The Windows Help window will open with the Contents tab displayed, as shown in **Figure 1-16**. Each of the major help topics covered is listed next to a book icon.

2 Position the pointer over Working with Programs in the Contents topics list. When you move the mouse pointer over the topic, the pointer will change to a hand, and the topic will be highlighted in blue and underlined, much like a Web page hyperlink.

3 Click Working with Programs. A list of subtopics will appear below it.

4 Click Start a Program. The help topic, including instructions, notes, and links to related topics, is loaded into the right half of the window for you to read (**Figure 1-17**).

5 Click the Index tab to bring it to the front of the left pane. The Index tab allows you to search the help files by keyword.

6 Type word processing. As you type, the list of topics will scroll to match your entry.

7 Click the subtopic WordPad to select it below the main topic word processing. Then click the Display button [Display]. Read the help text on Using WordPad that appears in the right frame.

8 Click ☒ to exit Help.

More

The Windows 2000 Help facility is written in HTML (Hypertext Markup Language). This is the same language used to create Web pages. Help's interface is similar to that of the Windows 2000 system windows, such as My Computer, and the Web pages you view with a Web browser. Across the top of the Help window are five buttons. Clicking the Hide button shrinks the Help window to only its right frame giving you more room to view other open windows. The Hide button changes to the Show button when the window is shrunk. The Back button takes you back to the topic you just viewed, while the Forward button takes you to the place you were before you clicked Back. The Options button offers you menu commands for the buttons, as well as others such as a print command and a stop command to interrupt long searches. The Web Help button gives you quick access to help on the Internet.

Figure 1-16 Windows help facility

Use Contents tab
to view help topics
by category

Click Search tab to
search help topics
for specific words
or phrases

Click Index tab to
view all help topics
in an alphabetized
list

Click Favorites tab
to add current topic
to Favorites list or
to go to help topics
added previously

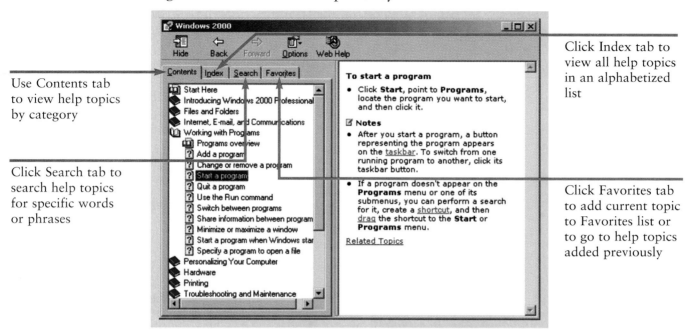

Figure 1-17 Help on WordPad

Help toolbar

Click a topic to
view its help file

Underlined text links
you to related help or
sometimes executes a
command when you
click it

Right frame of Help
window displays
selected help file

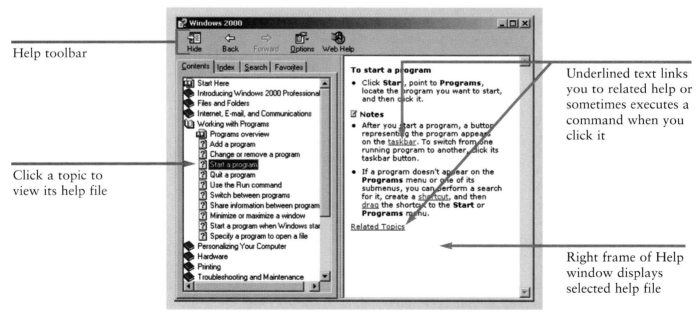

Practice

Get help on **printing a document** using
both the Contents tab and the Index tab.
Close the Help facility when you are done.

Hot Tip

The **Glossary** and **Reference** help topics
on the Contents tab are very useful for get-
ting help on specific Windows 2000 features that are not covered by the other
general help topics.

Shutting Down Windows 2000

Concept

It is important to shut down Windows 2000 properly. Failure to do so can result in loss of unsaved data. When you go through the shut down procedure, Windows 2000 checks all open files to see if any unsaved files exist. If any are found, you will be given the opportunity to save them. It also uses the shut down procedure to copy the data it has logged while your system was running to your hard disk.

Do It!

Shut down your computer to end your Windows 2000 session.

1 Click the Start button to open the Start menu.

2 Click Shut Down. A dialog box (**Figure 1-18**) will appear on your desktop.

3 A drop-down list in the center of the dialog box allows you to choose whether you want to log off the current user, shut down, or restart the computer. If the drop-down list box is set to Shut down, leave it as is. If not, click the arrow at the right end of the box, and then click Shut Down on the list that appears.

4 Click the OK button [OK]. Windows will go through its shut down procedure.

5 Turn off your computer when you see the message that reads: It is now safe to turn off your computer (**Figure 1-19**).

More

Table 1-2 Shut down options

SHUT DOWN OPTIONS	RESULT
Log off User	Ends the current session, but leaves the computer running so that another user may log on
Shut down	Prepares the computer to be turned off
Restart	Ends the current session, shuts down Windows 2000, and then starts Windows again

Figure 1-18 Shut Down Windows dialog box

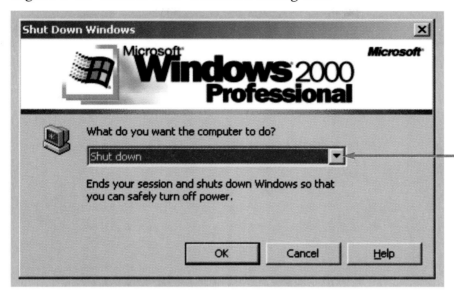

Click to select
another shut
down option

Figure 1-19 Shut down confirmation

Make sure all files and applications on your computer are closed, and then restart your computer.

You can also access the **Log Off** and **Shut Down** commands by pressing **[Ctrl]+[Alt]+[Delete]** on the keyboard to open the **Windows Security** dialog box.

Shortcuts

Function	Button/Mouse	Menu	Keyboard
Close window	☒	Click Control icon, then click Close	[Alt]+[F4]
Maximize window	☐	Click Control icon, then click Maximize	
Minimize window	▭ Or click program button on taskbar	Click Control icon, then click Minimize	
Restore window	▣	Click Control icon, then click Restore	
Change active window	Click window, if visible, or click program button on taskbar		[Alt]+[Tab]
Get Help on a specific item in a dialog box	?		[F1]

Identify Key Features

Name the items indicated by callouts in **Figure 1-20.**

Figure 1-20 Components of the Windows 2000 interface

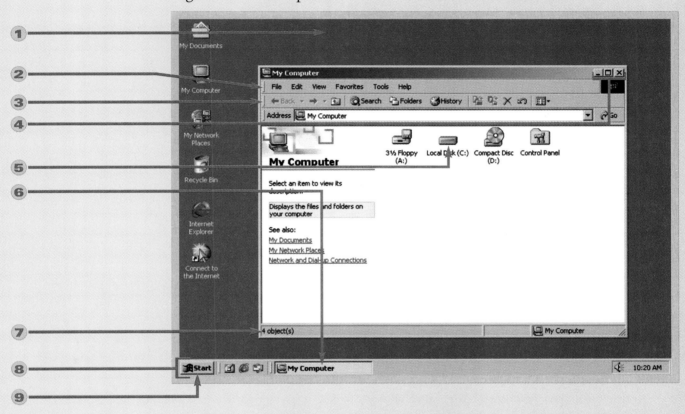

Select The Best Answer

10. Traditional way of opening a file, program, or window

11. Returns a maximized window to its previous size

12. Appears when a window is too small to display its information

13. Where you provide additional information before a command is carried out

14. Organizes the help files in major categories represented by book icons

15. Where program buttons appear

16. Used to manipulate the pointer on the screen

17. Minimizes all open windows

18. Contains a list of related commands

a. Scroll bar

b. Menu

c. Show Desktop button

d. Double-clicking

e. Restore button

f. Contents tab

g. Taskbar

h. Dialog box

i. Mouse

Quiz (continued)

Complete the Statement

19. All of the following are basic ways you can use a mouse except:

    a. Clicking

    b. Dragging

    c. Keying

    d. Pointing

20. You can move a window:

    a. When it is maximized

    b. By dragging its title bar

    c. When it is minimized

    d. By using the double arrow pointer

21. To open a context-sensitive pop-up menu:

    a. Click the mouse

    b. Click the Start button

    c. Double-click an icon

    d. Right-click the mouse

22. To scroll through a window in large increments:

    a. Click above or below the scroll bar box

    b. Click a scroll bar arrow

    c. Click the scroll bar box

    d. Right-click the Control icon

23. To locate a help file by means of a scrolling list that matches a topic you enter, use the:

    a. Contents tab

    b. Index tab

    c. Find tab

    d. Explorer tab

24. To reposition the taskbar:

    a. Open the Taskbar Properties dialog box

    b. Select it and press the arrow keys

    c. Drag it to a new location

    d. Right-click it and choose the Move command

25. A standard menu contains a list of:

    a. Related commands

    b. Shut down options

    c. Help topics

    d. Icons

26. Windows 2000's pictorial representation of a computer's functions and data is called:

    a. An IBI or "ibbey" (Icon Based Interface)

    b. A LUI or "louie" (Local User Interface)

    c. A HUI or "huey" (HTML Unified Interface)

    d. A GUI or "gooey" (Graphical User Interface)

27. An ellipsis after a command indicates that:

    a. Windows is still working

    b. The command is not available

    c. The command has a keyboard shortcut

    d. The command uses a dialog box

28. To open a menu, click on its title on the:

    a. Menu bar

    b. View menu

    c. Standard Buttons toolbar

    d. Keyboard

Interactivity

Test Your Skills

1. Start Windows 2000 and work with the desktop icons:

   a. If it is not already running, turn on your computer.

   b. Use the mouse to point to the My Computer icon.

   c. Move the My Documents folder icon to the center of the desktop, and then back to its original position.

   d. Open the My Documents folder icon.

   e. Close the My Documents window.

2. Work with an open window:

   a. Open the My Computer window.

   b. Move the window so that its title bar touches the top of the screen.

   c. Maximize the window.

   d. Restore the window.

   e. Use the mouse to resize the window until it is shaped like a square.

3. Run multiple programs and use the taskbar:

   a. Open Windows Explorer and Calculator from the Start menu.

   b. In turn, make each of the three open windows the active window.

   c. Minimize all open windows.

   d. Move the taskbar to the top of the desktop.

   e. Make the taskbar twice its original size.

   f. Return the taskbar to its original location and size.

   g. Close all open windows and applications

4. Use the Windows 2000 help facility and then shut down Windows:

   a. Open Windows Help.

   b. Use the Contents tab to read about What's New in Windows 2000.

   c. Use the Index tab to get help on printing help topics.

   d. Close the help facility.

   e. Shut down Windows 98 properly and turn off your computer.

Interactivity (continued)

Problem Solving

1. Using the skills you learned in Lesson 1 and your knowledge of the Windows 2000 operating system, arrange your desktop so that it resembles the one shown in **Figure 1-21**. Remember that computers can be configured in a number of different ways, and settings can be changed over time. Therefore, your setup, and the icons made available by it, may prevent you from replicating the figure exactly. Do not delete icons without consulting your instructor first.

Figure 1-21 Example of a Windows 2000 desktop

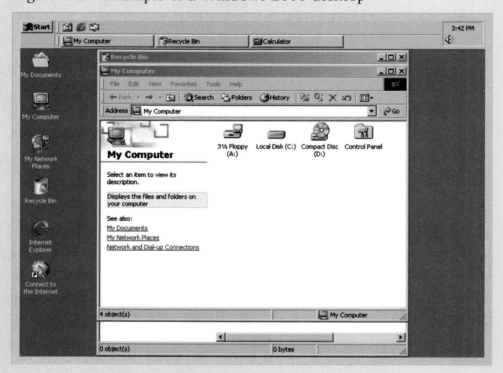

2. You have noticed an item on your Accessories menu named Notepad, but you are not sure what its function is. Use both the Contents and Index tabs in Windows 2000's Help facility to find out as much as you can about Notepad. Then use the Help facility to find out how to store the Notepad help topics you found on the Favorites tab. Once you have learned this procedure, add the most informative Notepad help topic to the Favorites tab.

3. You are working on a project that requires you to use two applications at the same time, Windows Explorer and Notepad. Open each application from the Start menu. Then resize and arrange the two open windows so that you can view them side by side on the desktop.

4. You are new to the Windows operating system, but you have used another operating system with a graphical user interface. You have decided to set up your desktop so that it resembles this system. Move all of your desktop icons to the right side of the desktop. Then move the taskbar so that it is anchored to the left side of the screen instead of to the bottom of it.

L E S S O N

2

MANAGING FILES WITH WINDOWS EXPLORER

A **file** is a text document, picture, or any other collection of information that is stored under its own unique name. A **folder**, much like a paper folder, is a collection of files that can also house other folders. Your computer stores electronic files and folders as you might store paper ones in a filing cabinet. To make finding files and folders easier, you should group them in an organized and logical manner. The manner in which your files and folders are arranged is called a **file hierarchy**.

A file hierarchy, as shown in **Figure 2-1**, is similar to a family tree. The parent, child, and grandchild branches are represented by disk drives and folders. A file hierarchy depicts all the drives, applications, folders, and files on your computer. Placing similar files into well-named folders is the best way to create a meaningful file hierarchy. By viewing the higher levels of your file hierarchy, you will be able to get a sense of where files are stored without having to open each particular folder.

My Computer and **Windows Explorer** are both file management tools. File management can be complex and even tricky at first. The key to understanding file management is being able to visualize and organize the placement of your files. Having to search through the entire file hierarchy every time you wish to locate an item can become time-consuming and frustrating. Learning how to manage your files effectively, by understanding My Computer and Windows Explorer, will help you to get the most out of your computer. My Computer and Windows Explorer are similar in function and in use. After a brief examination of My Computer we will concentrate on Windows Explorer, the more versatile file organizer.

Managing your files will often involve more than just organizing them. In this lesson, you will learn how to use the **Recycle Bin** to delete files and folders correctly. This will save you space on your hard drive and prevent you from disposing of important work accidentally. The lesson also introduces the **Search** command, which can help you locate a file when you lose track of it.

Viewing Folders with My Computer

Concept

My Computer is a tool that shows you the organization of the drives and configuration of folders on your computer. You can use My Computer to navigate through your system's files. Opening an icon in the My Computer window, usually for a drive or a folder, will show you that particular icon's contents. My Computer allows you to view the contents of your computer four different ways: by Large Icons, by Small Icons, in List form, or with Details. Once you open a drive or folder from the My Computer window, a fifth viewing option, Thumbnails, becomes available. How you view the contents of a drive or folder will depend on the information you require.

Do It!

To get a better understanding of file management, explore your C: drive by viewing its contents with the different View options.

1. Open the My Computer window by double-clicking its icon on the desktop (usually located in the upper-left corner of the screen).

2. To toggle between views, you need to make sure the Standard Buttons toolbar is visible. Open the View menu and guide the pointer onto the Toolbar command. If there is no check mark beside the Standard Buttons command, point to it and click the left mouse button.

3. The My Computer window displays icons that represent your computer's disk drives and system control folders. Double-click the C: drive icon ⊟ Local Disk (C:) to view the folders and files on your hard drive (your C: drive may have a different label than the one shown here). **Figure 2-2** shows the C: drive window in Large Icons view. This view takes up window space, but offers a clear view of a window's contents. By default, Windows 2000 enables Web content in folders, meaning the folders are presented like Web pages with frames and graphics. Evidence of this appears on the left side of the window, where the selected drive is named and a pie chart graphic depicts the drive's storage capacity in percentages of free and used space.

4. To view the items as Small Icons, click the Views button on the right end of the Standard Buttons toolbar ⊞▾. A menu will appear, shown in **Figure 2-3**, allowing you to select your choice of views. The bullet marks the current view, Large Icons.

5. Click Small Icons on the Views button menu. The icons will become smaller, and they will be arranged alphabetically in rows. This view is useful when you have many icons to fit into one window.

Figure 2-1 Sample file hierarchy

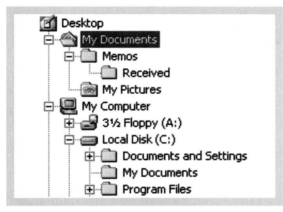

Figure 2-2 C: drive in Large Icons view

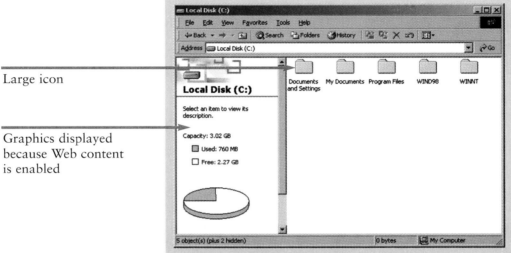

Large icon

Graphics displayed
because Web content
is enabled

Figure 2-3 Views button menu

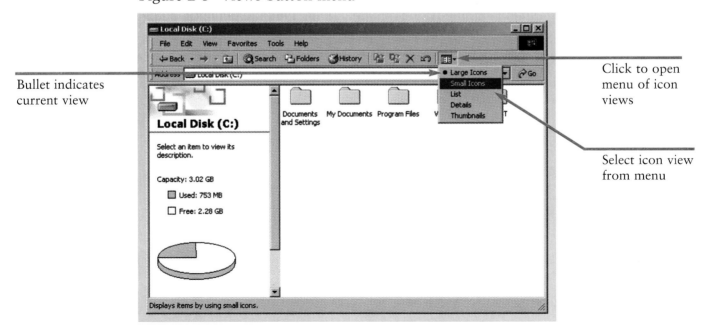

Bullet indicates
current view

Click to open
menu of icon
views

Select icon view
from menu

Viewing Folders with My Computer (continued)

Do It!

6 Click 🖳 again, then select List. The icons will be put into List view. List view is similar to Small Icons except that icons are organized in columns.

7 Click 🖳 again, then select Details. **Figure 2-4** shows Details view, which will tell you the name of an item, its size if it is a file rather than folder, its type, and even the last time you modified it.

8 To return to the top level of the hierarchy, click the Up button 🖿. The Up button steps you up one level in the file structure, while the Back button ⬅ Back returns you to the last file or folder you viewed regardless of its place in the hierarchy.

9 Right-click the title bar of the C: drive window, then select Close from the pop-up menu that appears to remove the window from the desktop.

More

As hard as you try, even with good file organization and file naming, it is impossible to remember what every file on your computer contains. Having Web content enabled in your folders can help relieve some of this frustration. Folders with Web content enabled allow you to see previews of file content, as well as get descriptions of hard drives and system folders. Compatible material includes Web pages, audio files, video files, and most graphic formats. When you select a file that can generate a preview, a small image of the file, called a thumbnail, will appear on the left side of the window, as shown in **Figure 2-5**. Thumbnails view allows you to view previews of all image files in a folder rather than file icons. Audio and video previews will contain controls for playing the particular file from the window without having to open another application.

The columns that are shown in Details view for a particular folder are determined by the Column Settings dialog box, which can be accessed by selecting the Choose Columns command from the View menu. The dialog box provides a list of column headings that are available for viewing and check boxes next to each heading to allow you to activate and deactivate the headings according to your needs and preferences. You can also alter the order in which the column headings appear, and specify their individual widths.

You can also customize the appearance of a folder by choosing the Customize This Folder command from the View menu. The command activates the Customize This Folder wizard, which will guide you through the steps required to choose or edit an HTML template for the active folder, change the folder's background picture and file name appearance, or add a comment to the folder.

The number and type of drives installed in a computer can vary greatly, but the configuration you have seen represented in this book is quite common. The drive designated with the letter A is almost always a 3½ inch floppy disk drive. The drive designated with the letter C is generally the computer's main hard drive. The D designation us usually assigned to the computer's CD-ROM drive. Traditionally, the letter B is reserved for a second floppy drive.

Figure 2-4 C: drive in Details view

Selected drive, folder, file, or Web address displayed in Address Bar

Click here to arrange folders and files alphabetically by name

Click here to arrange window contents by date last modified

Click here to sort window contents by file format

Click here to sort files by size

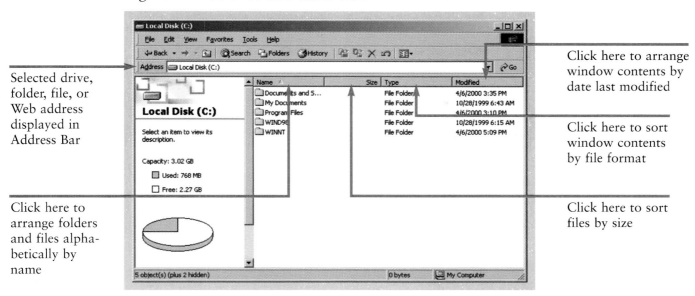

Figure 2-5 Preview of a bitmap image file

Details of selected file

Preview of selected file

Selected file

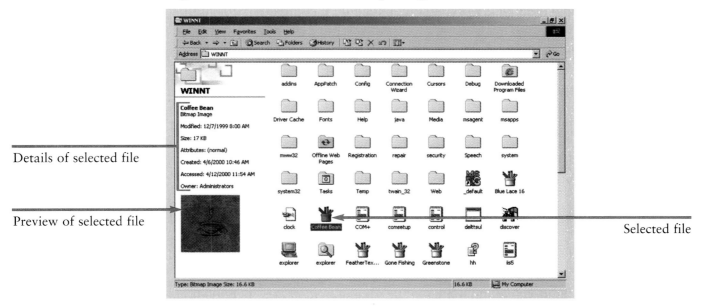

Practice

Open My Computer, double-click the Control Panel folder, then use the Views button to display the items in each of the available views. Leave the window in the view you like best. Close the window when you are finished.

Hot Tip

The My Computer and Control Panel windows are always displayed as Web pages. The Customize This Folder wizard is not available for these folders.

Using Windows Explorer

Concept

Windows Explorer, found on the Accessories menu in Windows 2000, is similar to My Computer. Both are file management tools that allow you to view the contents of your computer. But, Windows Explorer is more powerful and provides you with more options than My Computer. Windows Explorer displays itself as the two-paneled window you see in **Figure 2-6**, allowing you to work with more than one drive, folder, or file at a time. The left panel, which usually consists of the Folders Explorer Bar, shows all the folders and disk drives on your computer. The right panel, the contents panel, is a display of the items located within the folder or drive that is selected in the Folders Explorer Bar. This two-paneled window creates a more detailed view of a specific folder and makes for easier file manipulation, especially copying and moving.

Do It!

Use Windows Explorer to examine folders on your computer.

1. Click [Start], highlight Programs, highlight Accessories, and then click Windows Explorer on the Accessories menu. Windows Explorer will open with the contents of your computer shown in the left panel, and the My Documents folder selected. If you do not see the Folders Explorer Bar on the left, click the Folders button [Folders] on the Standard Buttons toolbar.

2. Click the plus symbol [+] next to My Computer in the Folders Explorer Bar (left panel). The [+] next to an item in this panel indicates that the item can be expanded to reveal its contents. You should now see the same drives and folders you saw previously in the My Computer window listed below My Computer in the left panel. Notice that the [+] you clicked has now changed to a [−]. This symbol indicates that a drive or folder is already expanded. Clicking the [−] collapses a drive or folder's contents back into the parent drive or folder. If a folder contains files but no subfolders, a plus sign will not appear next to it.

3. Click the [+] next to your C: drive in the Folders Explorer Bar to expand the drive, revealing its top level contents. The list of items you see in the left panel will differ from computer to computer depending on the files that have been installed and the way they have been configured.

4. Click the WINNT folder in the left panel. Now that the folder is selected, its contents, including subfolders and files, are displayed in the right panel (you may receive a message that explains the contents of the folder — if so, click the Show Files link that appears in the message).

5. Double-click the Media folder in the right panel to open the folder. You could have also expanded the WINNT folder in the left panel, and then clicked the Media folder there to display its contents in the right panel. Notice that the WINNT folder is now expanded in the Explorer Bar and the Media folder is shown with an open folder icon. The files inside the Media folder are sound files that were installed automatically with Windows 2000.

6. Press [Ctrl]+[A]. All of the items in the right panel will be selected, as shown in **Figure 2-7**. Pressing [Ctrl]+[A] is the keyboard shortcut for the Select All command on the Edit menu.

Figure 2-6 Windows Explorer

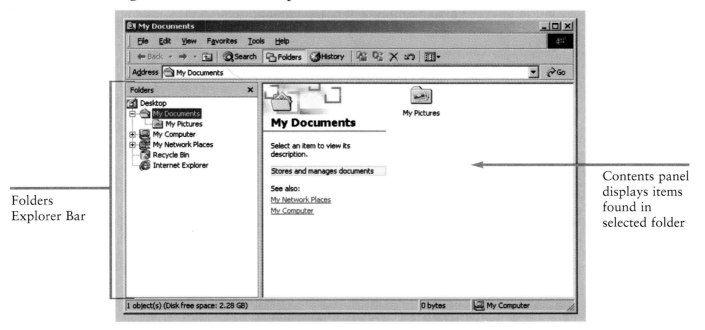

Folders
Explorer Bar

Contents panel
displays items
found in
selected folder

Figure 2-7 Media folder with all items selected

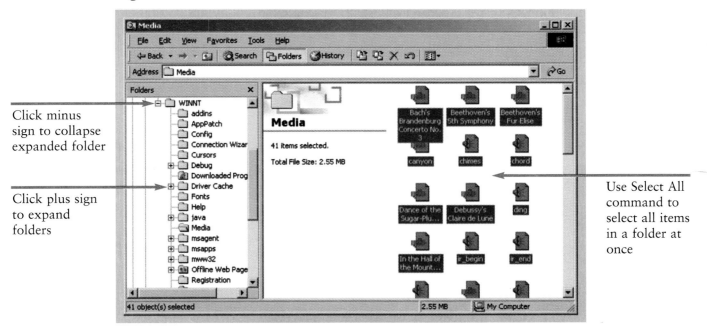

Click minus
sign to collapse
expanded folder

Click plus sign
to expand
folders

Use Select All
command to
select all items
in a folder at
once

Using Windows Explorer (continued)

Do It!

7 Switch to Small Icons view, and then press [End] on the keyboard The last file in the Windows folder will be selected. Since this is a sound file, audio controls appear in the window, allowing you to play the sound directly from Windows Explorer.

8 Press [Home] to select the first item listed in the Media folder.

9 Press [R] to select the first item in the folder that begins with the letter R. This is useful if you know the name of a file or folder and want to jump to it quickly.

10 Press [R] again to move to the next item in the list that begins with the letter R. Continuing to press [R] will cycle you through all the items in the folder that begin with R. Stop when you return to the first R item in the list.

11 With the first file that begins with R selected (most likely this will be recycle), hold [Ctrl] then click the file named chord. Holding the Control key down while you click allows you to select multiple, nonconsecutive files or folders.

12 Click the recycle sound file icon again to select it and deselect the chord file.

13 Hold [Shift], then click the first file listed. All of the files between the two you clicked will be highlighted, as shown in **Figure 2-8**. Holding the Shift key while you click allows you to select all of the items between the first and last selected.

14 Click a blank area to the right of the file names in the right panel to deselect all of the currently selected items. Leave Windows Explorer open for use in the next Skill.

More

Windows Explorer is a unique tool. As you saw in the Skill above, its two-paneled structure allows you to view all the folders on a specified drive, while working within a particular folder. One of the more powerful features of Windows Explorer is the left panel. The left panel, called the Explorer Bar, can be set to view one of four folders. By default, Windows Explorer opens in Folders view, which allows you to view any folders, files or utilities found on your computer or your network. The Search Explorer Bar, shown in **Figure 2-9**, allows you to activate Windows 2000's Search facility and locate files or folders directly in the Windows Explorer window. The Search Bar also contains a link that permits you to load an Internet search engine into Windows Explorer's left panel. If you would like to see a list of the locations you have visited recently, including local and network drives and Web sites, select the History Explorer Bar. Clicking the address or name of the place you want to view will load the site into the contents panel. You can choose to view items in the History Explorer Bar by date, site name, frequency of visits, or order visited today. The Favorites Explorer Bar allows you to store the places you visit most frequently so you can access them with a simple click. This feature is especially helpful with Web sites, which often have long, cumbersome addresses that are difficult to remember. You can close the active Explorer Bar by clicking the close button on its title bar, or by selecting the None command from the Explorer Bar submenu on the View menu.

Figure 2-8 Selecting multiple folders

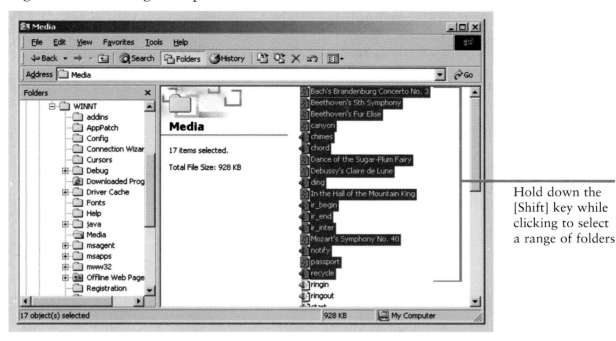

Hold down the
[Shift] key while
clicking to select
a range of folders

Figure 2-9 Search Explorer Bar

Open View menu
to select a different
Explorer Bar, or
click buttons on
toolbar

Enter search
criteria here

Click to load
Internet search
engine

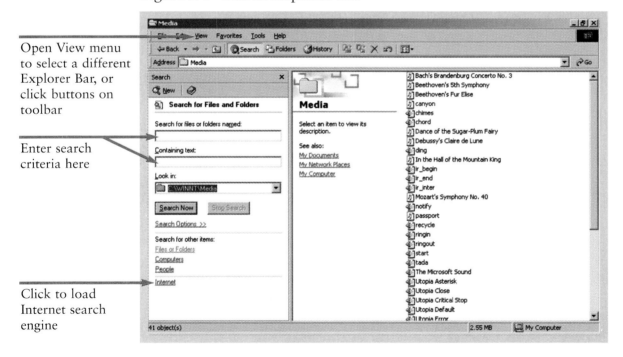

Practice

Expand the WINNT folder and select the
Fonts folder in the Folders Explorer Bar. The
files for all of the fonts installed on your
computer will appear in the contents panel.
Use the keyboard to select the font called
Verdana.

Hot Tip

You can resize the panels of Windows
Explorer. Place the pointer on the bar that
divides the window (it will change to ◄─►),
then drag to the left or right to resize the
bar.

Creating New Folders and Files

Concept

Creating folders is necessary when you want to store related files in a single location on a drive. Creating, naming, and placing folders properly in your hierarchy makes your work easier and more efficient. While most files are created in the program they will be used with, you can also make new, blank files right in the folder where they will be stored.

Do It!

Create a new folder on your C: drive, and then create another folder within that folder. Finally, create two new files in the folder that you made.

1 Expand the C: drive, and then click its icon in the left panel of Windows Explorer to view the items on your main hard drive in the contents panel on the right.

2 Click File on the menu bar. The File menu will open.

3 Guide the pointer to New, then click Folder on the submenu that appears. A folder with the default name New Folder will appear in the contents panel with its name highlighted, ready to be changed.

4 Type My Student Files, then press [Enter] to give the folder a unique name so you can find it again. Notice that the new folder also appears in the left panel.

5 Click the new folder's icon in the left panel of Windows Explorer to select it and reveal its contents. The right panel should be blank since this folder is empty.

6 Click File, point to New, then select Folder to create a new folder within your My Student Files folder.

7 Type Alice, then press [Enter] to name the new folder. The folder will be in the contents panel and a plus will appear next to My Student Files (**Figure 2-10**) in the left panel to indicate that at least one folder is nested within the parent folder.

8 Click the plus ⊞ next to the My Student Files folder in the Folders Explorer Bar to expand the folder and reveal the Alice folder nested inside.

9 Click File, select New, and then click WordPad Document on the menu that appears. A new file with the default name New WordPad Document will appear.

10 Type Letter.txt to rename the new file. Press [Enter] to confirm the file name. Creating a new file this way makes a blank document with a specific file format in the location you specify. The .txt at the end of the file name is an extension that tells the computer to associate the file with a particular program. By default, Windows 2000 associates the .txt extension with the Notepad program, but since this file was created as a WordPad document, it will open in WordPad when double-clicked.

11 Repeat the above step to create a WordPad document named To Do List.txt. Your window should look similar to the one shown in **Figure 2-11**.

Figure 2-10 Creating a new folder

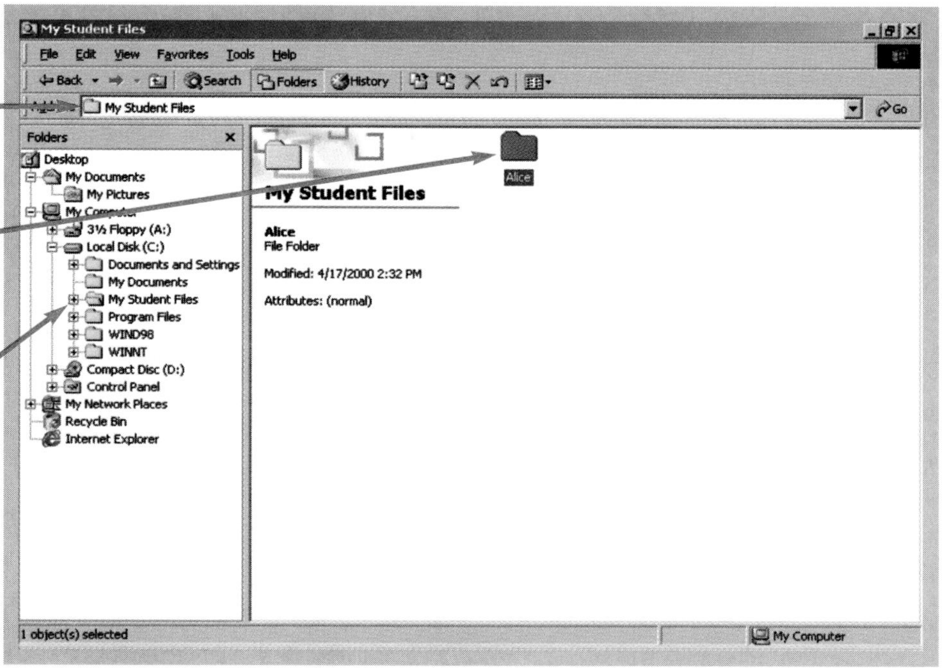

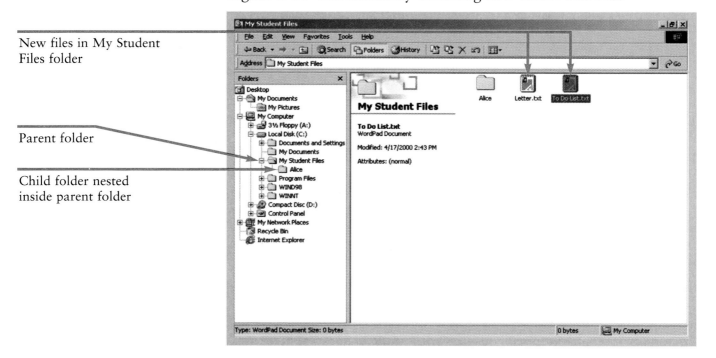

Name of selected folder

Alice folder created inside
My Student Files folder

Plus sign indicates that folder
may now be expanded to
reveal nested folders

Figure 2-11 File hierarchy including new folder and files

New files in My Student
Files folder

Parent folder

Child folder nested
inside parent folder

Creating New Folders and Files (continued)

More

New folders and files can also be created by right-clicking. Once a parent folder is selected, right-click a blank space in the right panel. A pop-up menu will appear, as shown in **Figure 2-12**. Highlight the New command on this shortcut menu, and a submenu will appear. By choosing the appropriate command from the submenu, you can make a folder or file just as you would using the File menu.

If you right-click a file or folder you will be given a different pop-up menu. **Figure 2-13** shows the menu that appears when you right-click on a file. The Open command opens the file with the application associated with the file's extension. The Open with... command allows you to choose a different application with which to open the file. The Print command lets you create a hard copy of the file without having to open the application with which it was created first. You can also use commands on the pop-up menu to cut, copy, delete, or create a shortcut to the file or folder you right-clicked. The Rename command allows you to change the name of the file or folder. Selecting a file or folder, pausing, and then clicking it again will also let you rename an item, as will selecting it and pressing [F2].

The pop-up menu that appears when you right-click a folder differs slightly from the file menu. It includes commands for opening the folder in Windows Explorer and setting network sharing options.

You can set options for each folder on your computer that control the way the folders appear and the way in which you interact with them. To do this, select a folder, open the Tools menu from the Menu bar, and then click the Folder Options command. The Folder Options dialog box, shown opened to the General tab in **Figure 2-14**, will appear. On the General tab, the Active Desktop section lets you determine whether Web content will be enabled on the desktop. The Web View section controls whether Web content is enabled in folders. The Browse Folders section is responsible for whether each folder you open appears in the same window or in a separate window. Finally, you can use the Click items as follows section to set your icon selecting and opening preferences: select by pointing/open by single-clicking (Web style) or select by single-clicking/open by double-clicking (traditional Windows style).

The View tab in the Folder Options dialog box contains advanced folder settings such as the option to display entire file paths in the Address Bar and the option to hide file extensions for known file types. The File Types tab is where associations between file types (extensions) and applications are set. The Offline Files tab allows you to make network files accessible when you are not connected to your network.

Figure 2-12 Right-click pop-up menu and submenu

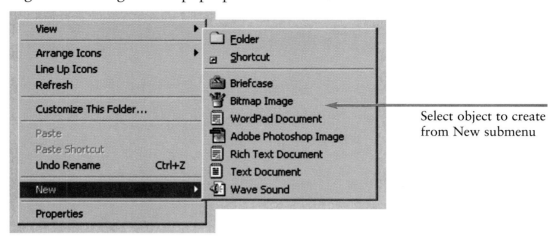

Select object to create from New submenu

Figure 2-13 Right-clicking a file

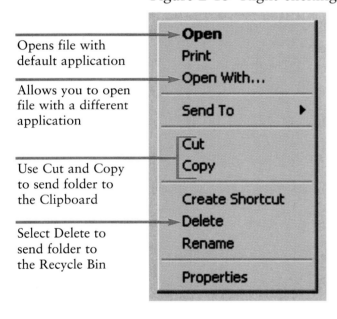

Opens file with default application

Allows you to open file with a different application

Use Cut and Copy to send folder to the Clipboard

Select Delete to send folder to the Recycle Bin

Figure 2-14   Folder Options dialog box

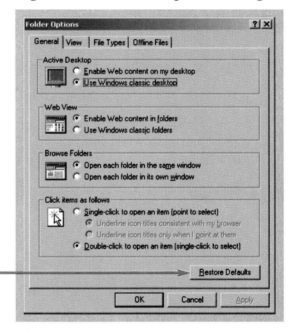

Click to restore Windows 2000's original settings

Practice

Create a folder inside the My Documents folder called **Practice**. Then create a new WordPad file called **Prac2-3.txt** inside this folder.

Hot Tip

Folder and file names can be up to 215 characters long so you can name your data accurately. The only characters you are not allowed to use are: \ / : * ? " < > |.

Moving and Copying Files and Folders

Concept

There are times when you will want to move and/or copy folders or files. Moving an item to group it with other files or folders that contain similar data can increase the overall efficiency of your work. Moving a folder changes its location and alters your file hierarchy accordingly. Copying a file or folder can be done to place a duplicate in another place on your system.

Do It!

Move the Letter and To Do List files into the Alice folder, and then make a copy of the Alice folder inside the My Student Files folder.

1. Open Windows Explorer using the Start menu if it is not already open.

2. Click your My Student Files folder in the left panel to select it (expand My Computer and the C: drive if necessary). The contents of the My Student Files folder, the Alice folder, Letter.txt, and To Do List.txt, will appear in the contents panel.

3. Click the ➕ next to the My Student Files folder so you can see the Alice folder in the left panel of Windows Explorer.

4. Hold down [Ctrl], while you click Letter.txt and To Do List.txt to select both files.

5. Drag the selected files from the right panel to the Alice folder in the left panel to move them. When you begin to drag, a faint outline of the files will follow the pointer. In certain areas, the pointer may become a circle with a line through it, indicating that you cannot drop your files at that particular location. You will know that the files are in the correct position when the Alice folder is highlighted, as shown in **Figure 2-15**. As soon as this occurs, release the mouse button to drop the files into the folder.

6. Click the Alice folder in the right panel to select it.

7. Click Edit to open the Edit menu, then select the Copy command to place a copy of the Alice folder on the Clipboard. The Clipboard is a temporary storage area in your computer's memory that holds copied or cut items until they are replaced on the Clipboard by another item or the computer is shut down.

8. Click Edit, then select Paste from the menu. A copy of the Alice folder will appear in the My Student Files folder as shown in **Figure 2-16**.

More

There are many ways to move and copy items in Windows 2000. Dragging and dropping files and folders from panel to panel in the Windows Explorer is one of the easiest ways to manage the information stored on your computer. Moving and copying can also be accomplished by dragging almost any item from your desktop to another system window or vice-versa. You can also move and copy with toolbar buttons. First, select the item you wish to move or copy. Then, click either the Move To 🖼 or Copy To 🖳 button on the Standard Buttons toolbar. In both cases, the Browse for Folder dialog box will appear, allowing you to choose a destination for the item to be moved or copied. Moving or cutting an item removes it from its original location. Copying leaves the original item in its original location.

Windows 2000

Figure 2-15 Moving files

Alice folder
highlighted,
ready to receive
files

Outline of files
being moved
attached to
mouse pointer

Selected files
being moved

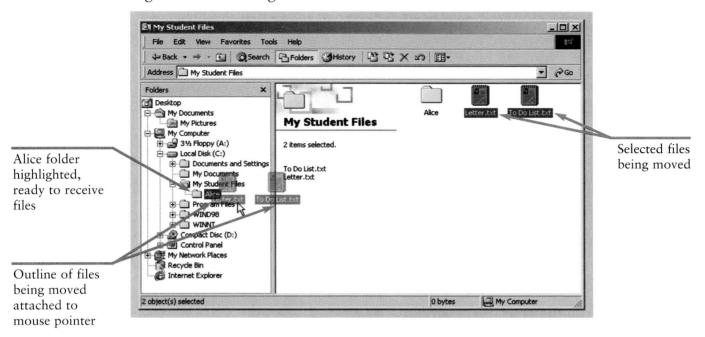

Figure 2-16 Copying a folder

Move To and
Copy To buttons

Copy of Alice
folder added to
hierarchy

Copy of Alice
folder in My
Student Files
folder

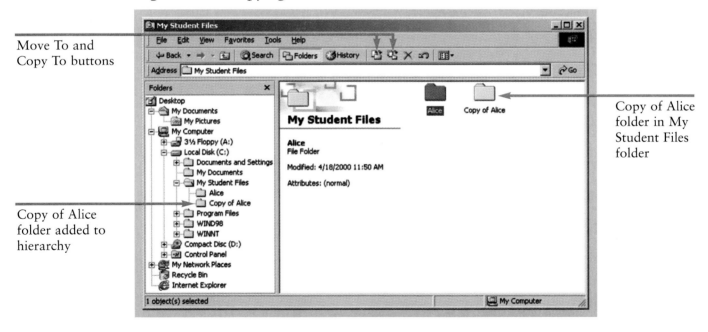

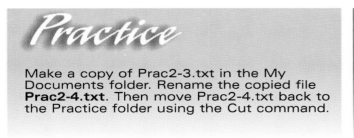

Practice

Make a copy of Prac2-3.txt in the My
Documents folder. Rename the copied file
Prac2-4.txt. Then move Prac2-4.txt back to
the Practice folder using the Cut command.

Hot Tip

Windows 2000 will not allow you to place
two files with the same name in the same
folder. If you attempt to do so, you will be
asked if you want to overwrite the first file
with the second. You may have files with
the same name in different folders.

Creating Shortcuts

Concept

Shortcuts are icons that give you direct access to frequently used items so that you do not have to open applications or folders in order to work with the item. Shortcuts can be created for programs, folders, files, Internet addresses, or even devices like printers. You can place shortcuts directly on the desktop or Start menu, or anywhere else you find convenient.

Do It!

Create a shortcut to the My Student Files folder on the desktop, rename it, and then change its icon.

1. Open Windows Explorer if it is not already running on your desktop.

2. If the Explorer window is maximized, click the Restore button so you can see a few inches of the desktop. You may have to resize the window so more of the desktop is visible.

3. Expand the appropriate icons so that the My Student Files folder is visible in the Folders Explorer Bar (left panel) of Windows Explorer. Place the mouse pointer over the folder's icon.

4. Right-drag (drag while holding down the right mouse button) the My Student Files folder to a blank space on your desktop. As the folder is dragged, a dimmed representation of it will move with the pointer. When you release the mouse button you will see the pop-up menu shown in **Figure 2-17**.

5. Click Create Shortcut(s) Here. A new folder named Shortcut to My Student Files will be created. The small arrow in the corner of the icon denotes that the folder is a shortcut, allowing you to access the My Student Files folder from the desktop without actually storing the folder on the desktop.

6. Right-click the Shortcut to My Student Files folder. A pop-up menu with commands relating to the folder will appear.

7. Click Rename. The folder's name will be highlighted so you can edit it.

8. Type To Be Deleted, then press [Enter] to rename the folder. **Figure 2-18** displays the shortcut with its new name.

Windows 2000

Figure 2-17 Right-dragging to create a shortcut

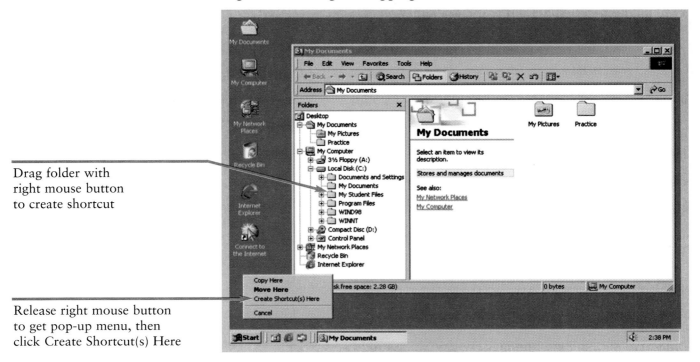

Drag folder with right mouse button to create shortcut

Release right mouse button to get pop-up menu, then click Create Shortcut(s) Here

Figure 2-18 Renamed shortcut folder on desktop

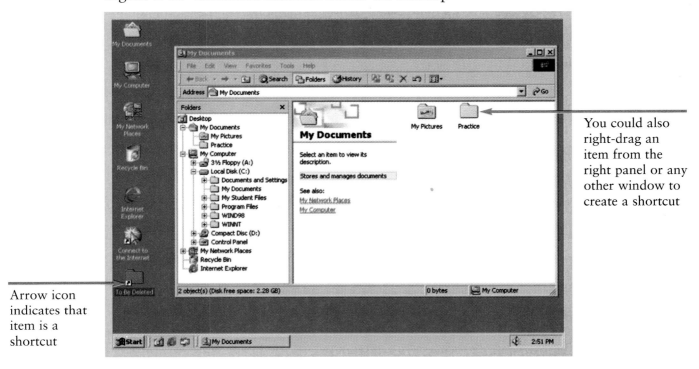

You could also right-drag an item from the right panel or any other window to create a shortcut

Arrow icon indicates that item is a shortcut

Creating Shortcuts (continued)

Do It!

9 Right-click the To Be Deleted folder, then select Properties from the pop-up menu. A dialog box (**Figure 2-19**) titled To Be Deleted Properties will open to the Shortcut tab. This tab contains data relating to the selected folder's shortcut properties.

10 Click the Change Icon button [Change Icon...]. **Figure 2-20** shows the Change Icon dialog box that will open.

11 Click and drag the horizontal scroll bar box to the right until the tree icon ♥ is visible.

12 Click the tree to select it.

13 Click [OK]. The Change Icon dialog box will close, returning you to the To Be Deleted Properties dialog box. The preview icon in the upper-left corner of the Shortcut tab will change to reflect your selection.

14 Click [OK]. The To Be Deleted Properties dialog box will close and the folder icon will be replaced with the tree icon, as shown in **Figure 2-21**.

More

Shortcuts can be made for many items stored on your computer, including files, folders, and drives that you access over a network. For example, you can make a shortcut to a frequently used folder that you access over a network for quick access to those files. Shortcuts do not have to be placed on the desktop either. You can create a folder of shortcuts to your favorite programs and place it on your C: drive, or even the Start menu.

As you have seen, many tasks can be accomplished using drag and drop techniques. One of the more powerful Windows 2000 features allows you to drag files to program icons. Doing so will open the file with the program whose icon you drop it on, assuming the file and application are compatible. For example, you can create a shortcut to your word processing program and place it on the desktop. Then, you can drag word processing files to that shortcut to open them. This also works with printers.

In the above exercise you changed the name and icon for the shortcut you created without altering the folder that the shortcut points to. While a shortcut points to a specific item, that object can be renamed without effecting the shortcut. However, target objects that are moved to another folder or drive will cause the shortcut to malfunction. If a target item is moved, Windows 2000 has the ability to find it, or you can specify the new path manually. Since shortcuts are icons that point to the actual file, folder, or program that they represent, deleting a shortcut will not effect the target item.

You can also create a shortcut by right-clicking an item and then choosing Create Shortcut from the pop-up menu that appears. The shortcut will be created in the same folder as the original item. You can then move the shortcut to the desired location. If you drag a shortcut to the Start button, the Start menu will open. You can drop the shortcut on the Start menu or any of its submenus.

Figure 2-19 Properties dialog box

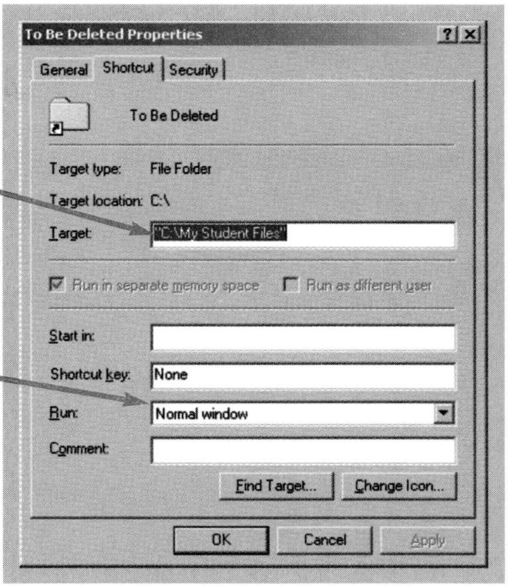

File path shortcut
follows to its target

Set shortcut to
open normal,
minimized, or
maximized
window

Figure 2-20 Changing an icon

Select an icon
to replace the
current one

Figure 2-21 Desktop shortcut with new icon

Renamed shortcut
with tree icon

Practice

Place a shortcut to the Practice folder on
your desktop.

Hot Tip

You do not have to be working in Windows
Explorer in order to create a shortcut. You
can also create shortcuts from the My
Computer window or any standard folder
window.

Using the Recycle Bin

Concept

The Recycle Bin is a storage place for files that have been deleted. Files that you no longer need should be deleted in order to save disk space and maximize the efficiency of your computer. If you decide that you need a file again, or have accidentally deleted a file, you can rescue it from the Recycle Bin. If you know you will never need a file again, you can delete the file permanently.

Do It!

Send the Copy of Alice and To Be Deleted folders to the Recycle Bin. Then rescue To Be Deleted from the Recycle Bin. Finally, delete both items from your hard drive permanently.

1. Open Windows Explorer from the Start menu.

2. Expand the necessary icons, and then click the My Student Files folder in the left panel to select it.

3. Click the Copy of Alice folder in the right panel, then click the Delete button [X] on the Standard Buttons toolbar. The Confirm Folder Delete dialog box (**Figure 2-22**) will appear, asking you if are sure you want to move the folder to the Recycle Bin.

4. Click [Yes]. The dialog box will close and the folder will be moved to the Recycle Bin. Notice the change in the Recycle Bin icon [🗑] when it is not empty.

5. Click the Close button [X] to exit Windows Explorer.

6. Click and drag the To Be Deleted shortcut from the desktop to the Recycle Bin [🗑]. When the Recycle Bin becomes highlighted, release the mouse button. The shortcut is deposited in the Recycle Bin.

7. Double-click the Recycle Bin icon. The Recycle Bin window will open. **Figure 2-23** shows the inside of the Recycle Bin displaying all the files and folder you have sent there.

8. Drag the To Be Deleted shortcut from the Recycle Bin window to an empty space on the desktop. The shortcut appears on the desktop, and is now an accessible item that can be used. Items still in the Recycle Bin cannot be opened.

9. Right-click the To Be Deleted shortcut and choose the Delete command from the pop-up menu to send the folder back into the Recycle Bin.

10. Click [Yes] to confirm the operation.

11. Click the Empty Recycle Bin button [Empty Recycle Bin] (if not visible click File, then click Empty Recycle Bin). The Confirm Multiple File Delete dialog box will appear.

12. Click [Yes] to delete the folders from your hard drive permanently.

13. Click [X] to shut the Recycle Bin window. Note that you can also empty the Recycle Bin by right-clicking it and then choosing the Empty Recycle Bin command.

More

Table 2-1 Ways to delete or restore a selected file

TO DELETE	TO RESTORE
Click the Delete button on the toolbar	Click the Undo button 🔄 on the toolbar
Right-click and select Delete from the pop-up menu	Right-click the file in the Recycle Bin and select Restore
Drag the file to the Recycle Bin	Drag the file from the Recycle Bin to any location
Press [Delete]	Go to the File menu in the Recycle Bin and select Restore or click [Restore]

Figure 2-22 Confirm Folder Delete dialog box

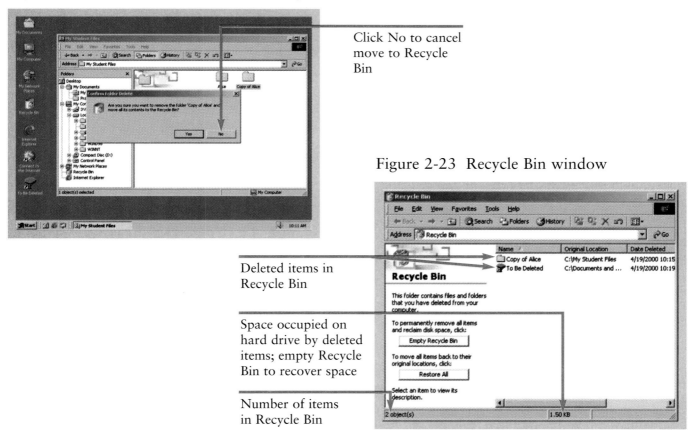

Click No to cancel move to Recycle Bin

Figure 2-23 Recycle Bin window

Deleted items in Recycle Bin

Space occupied on hard drive by deleted items; empty Recycle Bin to recover space

Number of items in Recycle Bin

Practice

Move the Practice shortcut you created in the last skill to the Recycle Bin. Then move the shortcut out of the Recycle Bin and back to the desktop. Delete the shortcut a second time using a different technique. This time, delete the shortcut permanently.

Hot Tip

Files can be erased immediately without being stored in the Recycle Bin. Right-click the Recycle Bin, then select Properties. On the View tab, uncheck the "Display delete confirmation dialog" command. This enables you to delete files in one step.

Searching for Files or Folders

Concept

Managing your files effectively includes knowing how to locate an item when you need it. The Search command on the Start menu is a tool that allows you to search your computer for files and folders when you do not know exactly where they are stored. You can also access the Search facility when working in Windows Explorer or My Computer by clicking the Search button 🔍Search to activate the Search Explorer Bar.

Do It!

Use the Search command to locate the Discover Windows 2000 tour.

1 Click 🏁Start, highlight Search, and then click For Files or Folders. The Search Results window, shown maximized in **Figure 2-24**, will open. The left side of the window contains the Search Explorer Bar. Near the top of the Explorer Bar is a text box in which you can enter the name, or a portion of the name, of the file or folder you wish to locate.

2 Type discover in the Search for files or folders named: text box. The Look in box should show your main hard drive. If not, click the arrow at the right edge of the box and select your main hard drive from the drop-down list.

3 Click the Search Now button Search Now. Windows will begin to search your computer's hard drive for any files or folders named discover. When the search is complete, the results will be displayed in the lower portion of the right panel (**Figure 2-25**). When your search is successful, you can open or run the item you have found by double-clicking it directly in the Search Results window. In this particular case, the item you have found is actually a shortcut and you would be prompted to insert your Windows 2000 CD-ROM in order to run the tour.

4 Close the Search Results window.

More

When you do not know the exact name of the file or folder you are looking for, you can use the wildcard character * in your search request. For example, if you search for all files or folders named J*, the search will return all files and folders whose names begin with the letter J. You can also use the Search Explorer Bar's Search Options feature when you do not know the file or folder name, or when you need to refine your search. When you click the Search Options link, the Search Options box opens in the Explorer Bar. The box contains four options: Date, Type, Size, and Advanced Options. Click the check box next to an option to use it. The Search Options box will expand to accommodate controls for the option you selected. For example, the Date option (**Figure 2-26**) allows you to search for files or folders that were last modified, created, or last accessed on a particular date or in a specific time frame. Setting such criteria can help narrow your search down to the items that will most likely satisfy your request.

Figure 2-24 Search Results window

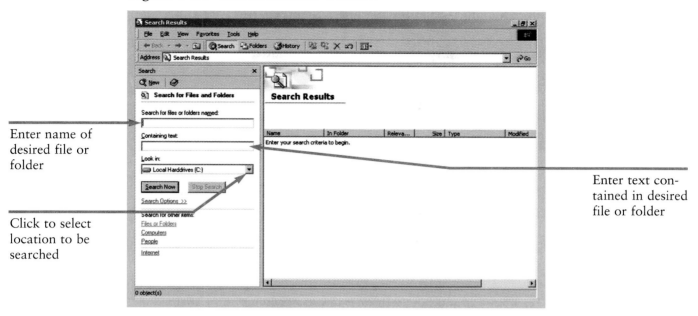

Enter name of desired file or folder

Click to select location to be searched

Enter text contained in desired file or folder

Figure 2-25 Results of search for discover

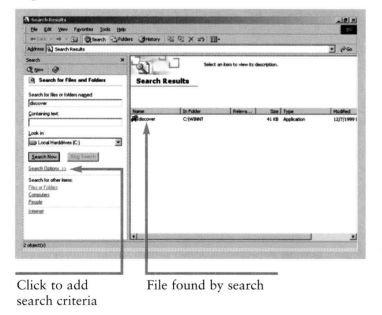

Click to add search criteria

File found by search

Figure 2-26 Date Search option

Practice

Use the Search command to locate your computer's Desktop folder.

Hot Tip

The Search menu and Search Explorer Bar also provide direct links facilities for Web page and people directory searches. You can even search for other computers located on your network.

Shortcuts

Function	Button/Mouse	Menu	Keyboard
Large Icons view	Click button, then click Large Icons	Click View, then click Large Icons	[Alt]+[V], [G]
Small Icons view	Click button, then click Small Icons	Click View, then click Small Icons	[Alt]+[V], [M]
List view	Click button, then click List	Click View, then click List	[Alt]+[V], [L]
Details view	Click button, then click Details	Click View, then click Details	[Alt]+[V], [D]
Thumbnails view	Click button, then click Thumbnails	Click View, then click Thumbnails	[Alt]+[V], [H]
Move up one level in file hierarchy		Click View, then highlight Go To, then click Up One Level	[Alt]+[V], [O], [U]
Move selected item to another folder		Click Edit, then click Move To Folder	[Alt]+[E], [V]
Copy selected item to another folder		Click Edit, then click Copy To Folder	[Alt]+[E], [F]
Cut selection to Clipboard		Click Edit, then click Cut	[Ctrl]+[X]
Copy selection to Clipboard		Click Edit, then click Copy	[Ctrl]+[C]
Paste selection from Clipboard		Click Edit, then click Paste	[Ctrl]+[V]
Delete selection		Click File, then click Delete	[Delete]
Undo last action		Click Edit, then click Undo	[Ctrl]+[Z]
Back	Back	Click View, then highlight Go To, then click Back	[Alt]+[Left Arrow]
Forward		Click View, then highlight Go To, then click Forward	[Alt]+[Right Arrow]

Identify Key Features

Identify the names and functions of the items indicated by callouts in **Figure 2-27**.

Figure 2-27 Standard Buttons toolbar

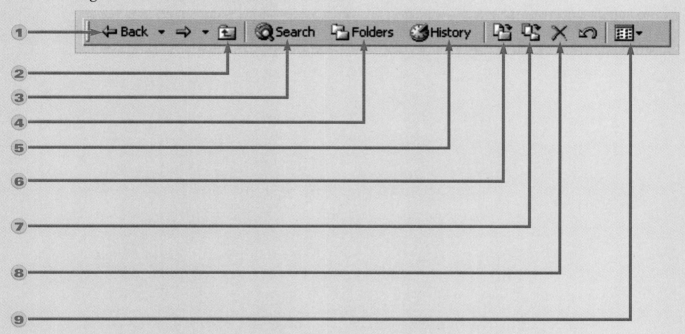

Select The Best Answer

10. Right side of the Windows Explorer window

11. One of the Explorer Bars

12. Allows you to relocate a selected file or folder

13. Storage place for deleted items

14. Its keyboard shortcut is [Ctrl]+[A]

15. An icon that gives you direct access to a frequently used item

16. Tool that allows you to view, open, and organize the contents of your hard drive

a. My Computer

b. Shortcut

c. Contents panel

d. Select All command

e. Folders

f. Move To button

g. Recycle Bin

Complete the Statement

17. A small arrow attached to the bottom-left corner of an icon signifies:

    a. A selected icon

    b. An expanded folder

    c. A shortcut

    d. A restored file

18. The temporary storage device that holds cut and copied items is called the:

    a. Recycle Bin

    b. Explorer window

    c. My Computer window

    d. Clipboard

19. Clicking the Views button:

    a. Automatically puts the icons in List view

    b. Automatically puts the icons in Large Icons view

    c. Opens the Views drop-down menu

    d. Cycles to the next view on the Views menu

20. To view information about the icons listed in a window, put the icons in:

    a. Details view

    b. List view

    c. The Recycle Bin

    d. The Windows folder

21. A plus sign next to a folder or drive in the Folders Explorer Bar indicates that it can be

    a. Collapsed

    b. Expanded

    c. Moved

    d. Deleted

22. A file in the Recycle Bin:

    a. Has been deleted permanently

    b. Can be opened by double-clicking it

    c. Can be restored by dragging it to a new location

    d. Must be copied and pasted to be restored

23. To find a folder by searching for its file type or file size, click the:

    a. Name & Location tab

    b. Search Options link

    c. Find Now button

    d. Find Now tab

24. The powerful two-paneled tool that allows you to work with more than one drive, file, or folder is:

    a. My Computer

    b. Windows Explorer

    c. The Recycle Bin

    d. The Create Shortcut dialog box

Interactivity

Test Your Skills

1. View the folders and files on your hard drive:

   a. Use **My Computer** to display the contents of your hard drive (C:).

   b. Put the contents of your hard drive in **Small Icons** view.

   c. Change to **List** view using the Menu bar.

   d. Return to the top level of the file hierarchy.

   e. Close the My Computer window without using the Close button.

2. Use **Windows Explorer** to view and select items on your hard drive:

   a. Open Windows Explorer.

   b. Expand **My Computer**, your **C:** drive, and then the **Program Files** folder.

   c. Select the **Internet Explorer** folder so that its contents are displayed in the right panel.

   d. Select all of the items in the contents panel.

   e. Select the **PLUGINS** folder in the contents panel without using the mouse.

   f. Select every other item in the contents panel.

   g. Select the last four items in the contents panel.

3. Create a new folder and a new file, then copy the file to another folder:

   a. Create a new folder on your C: drive (not in the Internet Explorer folder) called **TYS**.

   b. Make a **copy** of the folder.

   c. Create a new WordPad document called **TYS2.txt** in the original TYS folder.

   d. Place a **copy** of TYS2.txt in the My Documents folder.

4. Create a shortcut and practice using the **Recycle Bin**:

   a. Place a shortcut to the original TYS folder on your desktop.

   b. Send the **Copy of TYS** folder to the Recycle Bin without dragging it.

   c. Drag the **Copy of TYS2.txt** that you placed in the My Documents folder to the Recycle Bin.

   d. Empty the Recycle Bin.

Interactivity (continued)

5. Create a new shortcut and then use the Search feature to locate it on your hard drive:

   a. Place a shortcut to your C: drive on the desktop.

   b. Practice using the Search feature by locating the shortcut you just created.

   c. Open the shortcut from the Search Results window.

   d. Close all windows and delete the shortcut you created in step a.

Problem Solving

1. You have been running a successful guitar instruction business for several years now. Since your business continues to grow, you have decided to start managing it with a computer running Windows 2000. The first step of this project is to set up your hard drive with a system of useful folders. Start with a main folder called Business. Within the Business folder you should place a folder for each day of the week that you teach, Monday through Friday. Eventually, each of these folders will contain a folder for each student who has a lesson on that day. For now, each day of the week folder should hold a new WordPad document called [Insert day] Schedule.txt. Back inside the Business folder, create one text document with the name Student List.txt and another called Master Schedule.txt. Finally, place a shortcut to Master Schedule.txt inside each day of the week folder.

2. Your supervisor has asked you to be in charge of the New Media department's new multimedia software and documentation. Create a folder on your C: drive named New Media. Create two folders inside the New Media folder named Programs and Documentation. Open the Documentation folder and place a new WordPad document named Tech Support.txt inside the folder. Copy the document to your My Documents folder. Then rename the Programs folder you created Software.

3. Before you install Windows 2000 throughout your office, you want to review the software's end user license agreement, but you are not sure where to find it. Use Windows 2000's Search facility to look for a file named eula on your local hard disk. If you find it successfully, double-click the file in the Search Results window to open it. Then close the file and create a shortcut to it on your desktop.

L E S S O N

3

WORKING WITH INTERNET EXPLORER

Microsoft **Internet Explorer** is a software application that gives you the tools you need to take full advantage of the **World Wide Web**. Its integration with the Windows 2000 operating system makes it easy to browse the Web whether you want to find a local take-out restaurant, e-mail your sister to tell her about your new job, or find a message board relating to mandolins.

One of the most used facets of the Internet is the World Wide Web. It has increasingly become a key element of business, culture, community, and politics. You have already seen the browser window, as it is the same one used for My Computer and the Windows Explorer. The function of a browser is just that: it lets you browse, or surf, and view the pages that make up the Web. The World Wide Web is like a long hypertext document consisting of millions of pages that contain text, pictures, movies, and sounds. Among these pages you can find everything from information on NASA's latest launch to samples from your favorite musical artist's new CD.

When using Internet Explorer, most Web browsing can be done through a series of mouse clicks. Web pages are made up of **hypermedia**, which are words and pictures that are linked to other places on the Web and will transport you there when they are clicked. Internet Explorer also has toolbars that contain buttons to help you move through all the interesting material you will encounter on your journey across the Web.

As you wander around the Web you will encounter pages that you will want to return to later. To go to any page, all you need to do is remember the address (each Web page has its own), and then enter it into the text box provided on Internet Explorer's Address Bar. If you will want to visit a page often there is even a way to create direct links, or shortcuts, to your favorite Web sites. This is a good idea if a site's content changes frequently, such as that of a news service. The nature of the Web allows for frequent updating of a page's data. As you go through this book, keep in mind that a page's look or contents may have changed since the authors visited it. Some references may no longer be accurate when compared with what you view on your computer.

Introduction to the Internet

Concept

The Internet is an extended world-wide computer network that is composed of numerous smaller networks. In the late 1960s, the U.S. Defense Department's Advanced Research Projects Agency (ARPA) created a network of computers designed to withstand severe localized damage, such as that of a nuclear attack. Each computer on the ARPA network was connected to every other machine in such a way as to form a web. Each chunk of data sent from one machine to another was formatted as a packet, which also contained the address of where the packet originated and where it was headed. The web configuration and packet format enabled data to be rerouted if a node along its path in the network should be rendered inoperable. The packet-switching technology developed for ARPAnet became the foundation of today's Internet.

In the early 1980s, the National Science Foundation founded NSFnet, five supercomputing centers connected together on a network. Soon, other government agencies and educational institutions connected to NSFnet as well, adding information and infrastructure upon which an ever-larger network began to grow.

As more scientists, students, and computer enthusiasts became familiar with the Internet, more people began to log on from a variety of locations. **Figure 3-1** illustrates the phenomenal growth of Internet use. Soon, new software was developed to facilitate access to the Internet. Along with e-mail and newsgroups, two major uses of the Internet, the World Wide Web began to rise in popularity in the first half of the 1990s. The WWW is made possible by hypermedia and hypertext, objects such as pictures or lines of text that, when clicked, instruct the browser to go to another location on the Web. This allows for a nonlinear presentation of information, making the WWW, in effect, one huge hypermedia document made up of millions of individual files, each with their own address on the Web. The address at which a document is located on the Internet is called a Uniform Resource Locator or URL. A URL consists of three parts: the protocol (such as http or ftp), the location of the server on the Internet (domain), and sometimes the path to the requested data on the server's drive.

The Web works on a client-server model (**Figure 3-2**). The server, which is the computer containing the requested data, sends information to the client, the computer which receives it. The transfer of data between server and client follows a standardized protocol, or information exchange process. The Web standard is HTTP (HyperText Transfer Protocol), which allows all kinds of computers to understand and reliably translate hypertext Web files. Internet Explorer is a Web browser, which, like all Web software, conforms to HTTP standards. Web browsers are programs that allow a computer to translate the hypertext and display it. All Web browsers can read the text of all Web pages because these pages are written with a platform-independent language called hypertext markup language, or HTML. HTML documents consist of the text that will appear on the page, formatting instructions, and references to other files such as graphics that will be displayed on the page. The World Wide Web has become the most popular feature of the Internet, providing access to an almost unimaginable diversity of information.

Figure 3-1 The growth of the Internet

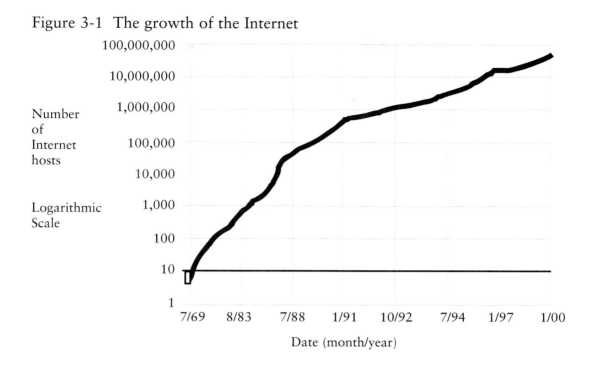

Number
of
Internet
hosts

Logarithmic
Scale

Figure 3-2 Clients and servers on the World Wide Web

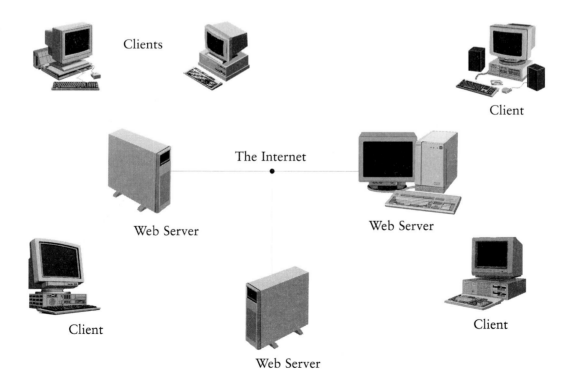

Opening Internet Explorer

Concept

Before you can begin surfing the Web with Internet Explorer (IE), you must open the application. You can accomplish this task in a variety of ways including using the Start menu, the Quick Launch toolbar, or a desktop icon. This skill assumes that you have a valid Internet connection and that your Web browser has been configured correctly. If this is not the case, begin by double-clicking the Connect to the Internet icon 🌐 on your desktop to launch the Internet Connection Wizard (also available on the Start menu: Programs/Accessories/Communications), which will guide you through the steps necessary to set up your Internet account and browser. Once you have run the Wizard, its shortcut icon will be removed from the desktop.

Do It!

Open Internet Explorer and then guide the pointer over the various parts of the window to become familiar with its interface.

1. Click the Internet Explorer quick launch icon 🅴 , located next to the Start button, to open the Internet Explorer window. Assuming that your connection to the Internet is valid, Internet Explorer will open. A page will appear in the browser window, which is shown maximized in **Figure 3-3**. This is called the browser's home page, and refers to the document that loads automatically when the application is launched. IE's default home page is the Microsoft Network's (MSN) home page, http://www.msn.com. (In this instance, the term home page refers to the main page of Microsoft's Web site.) Since Windows allows for customization, your browser window may be different than the ones shown, and your startup procedure may vary slightly from the one demonstrated here. For example, you may have to through a dial-up procedure if you are connecting to the Internet with a modem.

2. Internet Explorer's browser window resembles the standard Windows 2000 system window with which you are already familiar. You will notice the most change in the Standard Buttons toolbar. **Table 3-1** explains some of the features of this toolbar and how they allow you to use IE most effectively.

More

Changing your browser's home page is a relatively simple procedure. Open the Tools menu from Internet Explorer's Menu bar and click the Internet Options command. The Internet Options dialog box will open to the General tab. The top section of the General tab is titled Home page, and it contains a text entry box that holds the Web address for your browser's current home page. This address will be selected automatically when the dialog box opens. You can type any Web address to replace the one that is already there. Then click ▐ OK ▌ to confirm the adjustment and close the dialog box. The next time you open your browser or click on the Home button, the Web page whose address you provided will appear in your browser window.

If you have difficulty remembering the functions of the different toolbar buttons, you can customize the Standard Buttons toolbar so that it displays text labels for all buttons. To do this, right-click the toolbar, and then click the Customize command on the menu that appears. Near the bottom of the Customize Toolbar dialog box is a drop-down list box labeled Text Options that allows you to choose text labels for all button, selected buttons, or no text labels. The main part of this dialog box permits you to change which buttons actually appear on the toolbar.

Figure 3-3 Internet Explorer opened to MSN home page

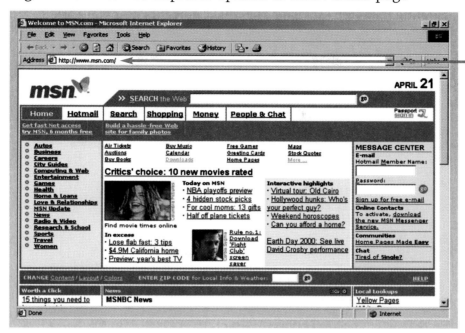

Address (URL)
of current Web
page displayed
in Address Bar
text box

Table 3-1 IE Standard Buttons toolbar

BUTTON	FUNCTION
⊗	Stops the loading of a page into the browser window
🔁	Reloads the current page; especially useful for pages that update frequently
Search Favorites History	Activates the corresponding Explorer Bar in the browser window
⌂	Loads the browser's home page into the browser window; the home page can be set on the General tab of the Internet Options dialog box
✉▾	Opens a menu of commands related to working with e-mail
🖨	Instructs a printer properly connected to your computer to print a copy of the current page

Practice

Change your browser's home page to the following address:
http://www.theglobe.com

Hot Tip

To restore your browser's original home page setting, open the Internet Options dialog box from the View menu. Then click the **Use Default** button in the Home page section of the General tab.

 # Navigating the Web

Concept

Since information on the Web is not presented in a strictly linear fashion, it is possible to follow links in any order you like, examining whatever you wish in more detail. This is often referred to as browsing or surfing. Most Web browsing with Internet Explorer is done using a few basic actions and controls.

Do It!

Practice moving around the Web using hyperlinks, navigation buttons, and the Address Bar.

1 From the MSN home page, you can gain access to news, free e-mail, reference materials, online shopping, and much more. Clickable words and images on the page are called hyperlinks. Position the pointer over the Hotmail link. The pointer will appear as a hand with a pointing finger 🖑 when over the link, indicating that it is an active link. The underlined text may also change color to red.

2 With the pointer still over Hotmail, click the left mouse button. The Microsoft Windows icon at the right end of the Menu bar will animate to indicate that the page you have requested is loading. The page should appear in the browser window momentarily, as shown in **Figure 3-4**.

3 Locate and click the Terms of Service link. You will be transported to a page that explains the terms of service for Hotmail®, Microsoft's free Web-based e-mail service. Notice that since you started following links, the Back button on the Standard Buttons toolbar has become active. Use the scroll bar to read text that is not visible.

4 Click the Back button `← Back` to go back to the previously viewed page, the main Hotmail page.

5 Click the Forward button `→`. The Terms of Service page reappears in the window. The Forward button only becomes active once the Back button has been clicked, and reverses the Back command.

6 Position the pointer in the Address Bar text box, and then click once. The URL (Uniform Resource Locator) of the current page will be selected.

7 Type http://www.altavista.com to enter this address manually, then press [Enter]. The home page of the AltaVista search engine, shown in **Figure 3-5**, will appear.

8 Click the Home button `⌂` to go back to your browser's home page.

More

The Forward and Back buttons both have small black downward-pointing arrows on their right edges. These arrows indicate that the button has a drop-down menu associated with it. If you click the arrow with the left mouse button, a list of recently visited pages appears below the button with the most recent at the top. Using this list allows you to quickly go back to a previously visited page without having to click the Back button repeatedly. In the same way, the Forward button's drop-down list shows sites that can be visited by clicking the Forward button. Right-clicking the Back or Forward button will also bring up these menus.

Figure 3-4 Microsoft's Hotmail® page

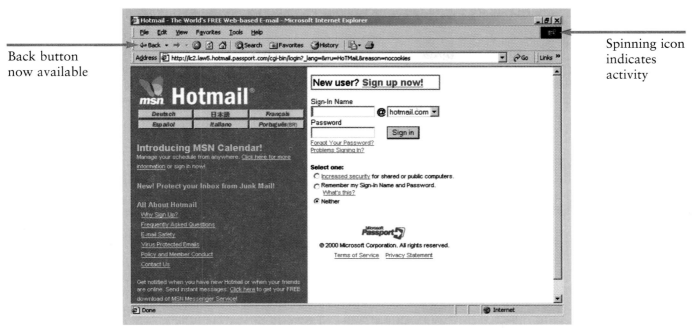

Back button
now available

Spinning icon
indicates
activity

Figure 3-5 Using the Address Bar to enter a URL

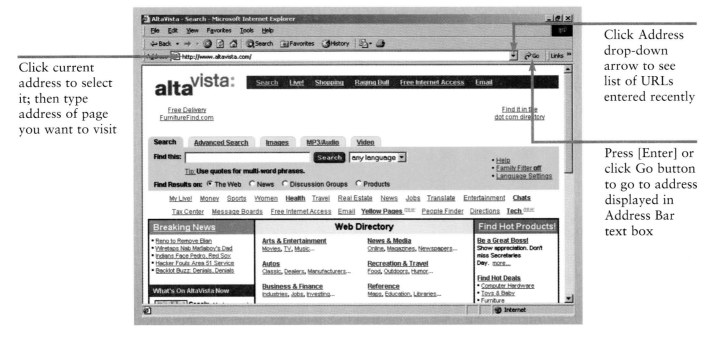

Click current
address to select
it; then type
address of page
you want to visit

Click Address
drop-down
arrow to see
list of URLs
entered recently

Press [Enter] or
click Go button
to go to address
displayed in
Address Bar
text box

Practice

Visit the Web page found at
http://www.usps.gov. Then use the toolbar to return to your browser's home page.

Hot Tip

Clicking the History button [History] on the
toolbar opens the History Explorer Bar on
the left side of the browser window. The
History Bar lists all of the pages you have
visited recently as hyperlinks so you can
revisit them with a single click.

Searching the Internet

Concept

There is an inordinate amount of information on the Internet. Being able to find what you want will help make your experience surfing the Web more productive and enjoyable. With Internet Explorer's Search Explorer Bar, you can retrieve and display a list of Web sites related to your topic of interest, and then load the actual Web pages into the same window. This convenience prevents you from having to navigate back to your search page each time you want to follow a different link.

Do It!

Use the Search Explorer Bar to find a Web site that offers used cars listings.

1. Click the Search button. The Search Explorer Bar (**Figure 3-6**) will appear in the browser window. Notice that Internet Explorer's Search Bar differs from the one you saw in Windows Explorer. This one is configured for Internet searches rather than for finding files or folders, though a link for searching for files or folders is still provided.

2. The default search category is Find a Web page, and the Find a Web page containing: text-entry box is ready to receive your search query. Type "used cars" (include the quotes). Enclosing the phrase in quotation marks instructs the search engine to treat the words you enter as a single unit and only search for pages that contain used and cars next to each other in that order. If the keywords are not enclosed in quotation marks, the search will return any pages that simply contains either word.

3. Click the Search button. The MSN search engine lists links to the 10 Web pages that will most likely satisfy your needs, determined by factors such as proximity of the words to each other and to the top of the page. If you point to a link, you will receive a ScreenTip that includes a description of the page and its URL.

4. Click a link from the list of results to visit that page. The site will load in the right panel, while the search engine remains in the left panel so that you can select another link, as shown in **Figure 3-7**.

5. To view the page in the entire window, click the Search button again to hide the Explorer Bar. The current search will remain in the Search Bar until you close Internet Explorer or click the Search button again to begin a new search.

More

Once you click a link in Internet Explorer, the link will change color so that you know you have already visited it. This is very helpful when you are working with a list of links such as that in the Search Explorer Bar. Most searches will return more than 10 results. If the first ten do not satisfy your needs, you will find a link below them that allows you to view the next set of links that match your search criteria. If you still aren't successful, you can try using a different search engine by clicking the Next button near the top of the Explorer Bar. If you want to choose a specific search engine, click the arrow on the right end of the Next button to open a menu of search engines. Clicking the New button reloads the basic Search Explorer Bar (**Figure 3-6**) so you can choose a new category of search. Clicking the Customize button allows you to choose which engines and directories will be used for each search category and the order in which they will be activated by the Next button.

Figure 3-6 Internet Explorer's Search Explorer Bar

Select a search category

Enter search words here

Click button to begin search

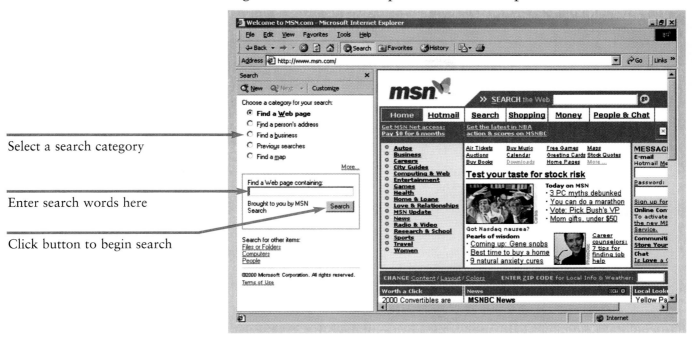

Figure 3-7 Using search results

Click to select a different search engine

Visited link changes color

List of links found as a result of search

Right panel displays selected Web page while search results remain in Explorer Bar

Practice

Use the Search Explorer Bar to find Web pages that will allow you to consult airline flight schedules. Then follow one of the links produced by your search.

Hot Tip

Most search engines are only case sensitive with uppercase letters. For example, a search for **Bugs Bunny** will return sites relating to the cartoon character, while a search on **bugs bunny** will result in a list of sites on insects and rabbits as well.

Creating Favorites

Concept

Internet Explorer allows you to make direct links, or shortcuts, to your favorite Internet sites so that you may revisit them easily without having to remember long URLs. This is also known as bookmarking. The Favorites menu offers several options for adding, organizing, and managing your favorites. Shortcuts to frequently visited sites may also be placed on the Links toolbar, on the desktop, or in a folder on your hard drive.

Do It!

Create a Favorite for a search engine, search for a site that contains a local weather forecast, and then place a shortcut to that site on the Links toolbar.

1. Click the Address text box to select its contents.

2. Type www.excite.com to replace the current URL, then press [Enter]. Internet Explorer automatically adds the protocol http://, and the Excite search engine/Web guide loads into the window.

3. Open the Favorites menu from the Menu bar, then click Add to Favorites. The Add Favorite dialog box will appear, as shown in **Figure 3-8**.

4. Click [OK] to create the favorite with the default settings and close the dialog box. The shortcut to the Excite page will be added to your Favorites list.

5. Open the Favorites menu to see that your shortcut is there. Then click the Favorites menu title again to close the menu.

6. Click in Excite's search text-entry box to place an insertion point there.

7. Type +weather +*the name of your city*. This instructs the search engine to look for sites that contain both of the words. If the plus signs had been omitted, sites containing either of the words, but not necessarily both, would be found.

8. Click [Search] to initiate the search (If a dialog box appears, click Yes to proceed).

9. Look through the list of matches, using the vertical scroll bar to advance the page as you go. Visit the sites that appear relevant to the original search objective by clicking their hyperlinks. Look for a site with a good local forecast. Use the Back button to return to the search results page to view additional found sites. When you find a site you like, stay there.

10. Assuming your Links toolbar is just visible at the right end of the Address Bar, drag the Links toolbar straight down so that it occupies its own row.

11. Click and hold the IE page icon 🗐 in the Address text box, and then drag it down to the Links toolbar. As you drag, the pointer will appear as an arrow with the shortcut arrow icon attached. A marker will appear in the Links toolbar indicating the place where the new Favorite will be created (only when you are between buttons or at the ends of the toolbar). When you release the mouse button a button for the current site will appear on the Links toolbar (**Figure 3-9**). A Favorite will also be added to the Links folder on the Favorites menu.

More

The Favorites that you create will not only appear on the Favorites menu in the Internet Explorer window, but everywhere the Favorites folder is accessible. This can include the Start menu and the Favorites menu in any system window. The Favorites that you create will be also be added to the Favorites Explorer Bar, which can be left open while you browse the Web for quick access to your shortcuts.

Figure 3-8 Add Favorite dialog box

Default favorite name taken from page title

Click to create favorite on different level of Favorites hierarchy

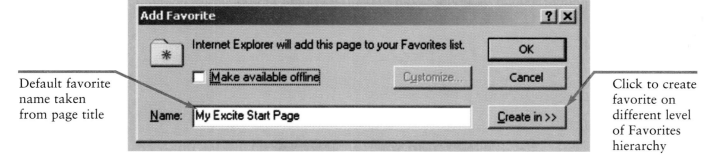

Figure 3-9 Adding a favorite to the Links toolbar

New button on Links toolbar

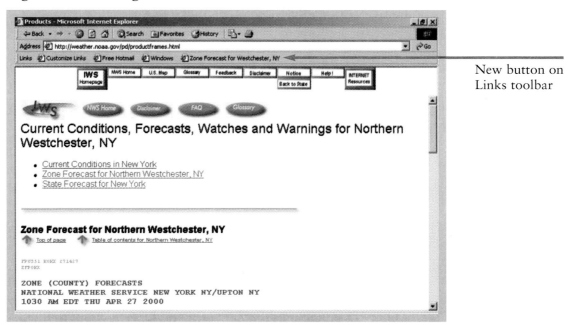

Add **www.amazon.com** to your Favorites folder. Then add **www.usps.gov** to your Links toolbar

You can drag any link on a page to create a shortcut just as you would to create it with the IE page icon. Dragging a link to the Links toolbar, for example, will create a shortcut for that link rather than the currently displayed Web page.

 # Managing Favorites

Concept

Without sufficient attention to organization, a long list of Favorites can be difficult to manage. By editing and grouping Favorites, you can make them much easier to use. Internet Explorer allows you to create or delete folders on the Favorites menu, redistribute Favorites among the folders, and rename Favorites and the folders that hold them.

Do It!

Create a new folder that will store your personal Favorites, move a Favorite into that folder, and then rename the Favorite.

1. Click Favorites on the Menu bar, then click the Organize Favorites command. The Organize Favorites dialog box will open, as shown in **Figure 3-10**.

2. Click the Create Folder button [Create Folder]. A new folder will be created in the Organize Favorites dialog box with its default name selected, ready to be changed.

3. Type Search Engines, then press [Enter]. The name of the folder will change, and the folder will remain selected.

4. Click the favorite you created for the Excite page in the last skill to select it. Notice that its properties are displayed in the bottom-right corner of the dialog box.

5. Click the Move to Folder button [Move to Folder...]. The Browse for Folder dialog box will open.

6. Click the Search Engines folder you created to select it as the destination folder to which you will move the Excite favorite. When you select the folder it will be highlighted and appear as an open folder, as shown in **Figure 3-11**.

7. Click the OK button [OK]. The Browse for Folder dialog box closes, and the selected favorite is moved.

8. Click the Search Engine folder to show its contents in the dialog box.

9. Click the Excite Favorite to select it.

10. Click the Rename button [Rename]. The Favorite's name will be highlighted.

11. Type Excite.com, then press [Enter] to rename the Favorite, as shown in **Figure 3-12**. Close the Organize Favorites dialog box.

More

In the previous Skill you created a Favorite on the top level of the Favorites hierarchy. The Favorites folder is the default location for creating shortcuts. If you click the Create In button the dialog box will expand, showing you a pane in which the current Favorites hierarchy is displayed. This pane is similar to the Browse for Folder dialog box pictured in **Figure 3-11**. From this additional pane you can select the folder in which you wish to create the new Favorite, thereby eliminating the process of moving it later.

Figure 3-10 Organize Favorites dialog box

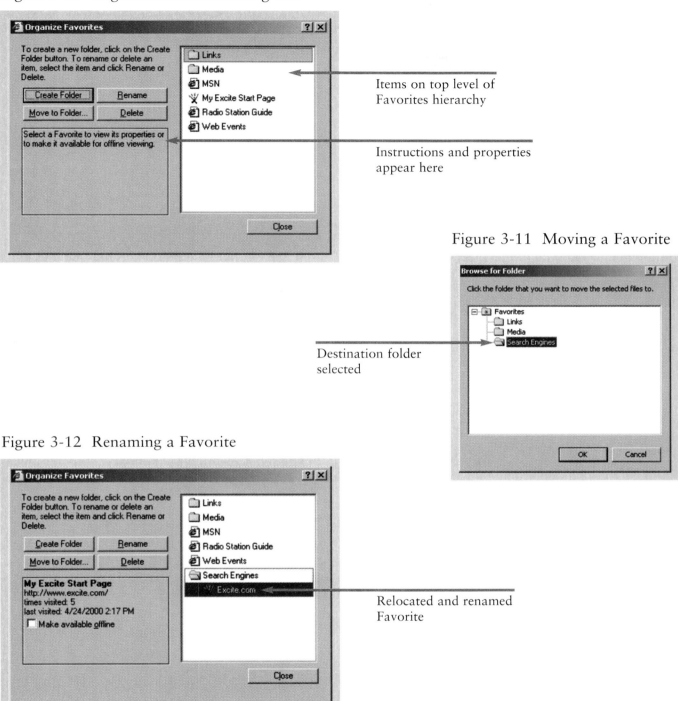

Items on top level of
Favorites hierarchy

Instructions and properties
appear here

Figure 3-11 Moving a Favorite

Destination folder
selected

Figure 3-12 Renaming a Favorite

Relocated and renamed
Favorite

Practice

Create a new Favorites folder called **Online Shopping**. Then move the Amazon.com Favorite you created in the previous Practice exercise into this new folder.

Hot Tip

You can use the drag and drop technique to move Favorites from folder to folder inside in the Organize Favorites dialog box. Right-clicking an item will allow you to rename it.

Printing a Web Page

Concept

In general, Web pages are designed primarily for on-screen viewing. However, there may be occasions when you want to print a paper copy of a particular page. In fact, most online shopping sites suggest that you print your transaction page when you have completed a purchase so you can keep it for your records. In addition, many software and hardware manufacturers provide installation instructions online that you can print and then follow as you install new software.

Do It!

Use Internet Explorer's Print command to print a paper copy of a Web page.

1 Use the Favorite you created earlier to go to www.excite.com.

2 Click File to open the File menu, then click the Print command. The Print dialog box, shown in **Figure 3-13**, appears with the General tab in front.

3 If your computer is connected to more than one printer, you can select the icon for the printer you wish to use in the Select Printer section of the dialog box.

4 When the correct printer is selected, click ⬛ Print to print the Web page with the default settings. Your printer should print one copy of the page, but it might require more than one piece of paper to do so since Web pages are not necessarily designed to fit on standard paper sizes.

More

Even though Web pages are designed for the screen rather than paper, you do have some control over how a page will appear when you print it. Before you print, open the File menu and choose the Page Setup command. The Page Setup dialog box will open, as shown in **Figure 3-14**. In the Paper section of the dialog box, you can select the size of the paper you are printing on and how it is being fed into the machine. These options are also available on the Paper Quality tab in the Print dialog box. In the Headers and Footers section, you can specify text that will appear at the top and bottom of the printed page. The Orientation section determines whether the page will be printed like a traditional document (Portrait), or so that its left to right length is greater than its top to bottom length (Landscape). Page orientation can also be controlled form the Layout tab in the Print dialog box. Finally, you can set the distance for all four of the page's margins in the Margins section.

Some Web pages are divided into separate components known as frames. When you print a page that uses frames, the Print frames section of the Print dialog box (**Figure 3-13**) will be active. From here you can choose to print the page exactly as it appears on your screen, print a single frame that you select, or print each frame individually. Just below the Print frames section are two check boxes. The first instructs your printer to print all documents that are linked to the one you are currently printing while the second simply adds a table of these links to the end of the printout. These items are also available on the Print dialog box's Options tab.

You can bypass the Print dialog box by clicking on the Print button 🖨 on the Standard Buttons toolbar. Your document will be printed using the current print settings.

Figure 3-13 Print dialog box

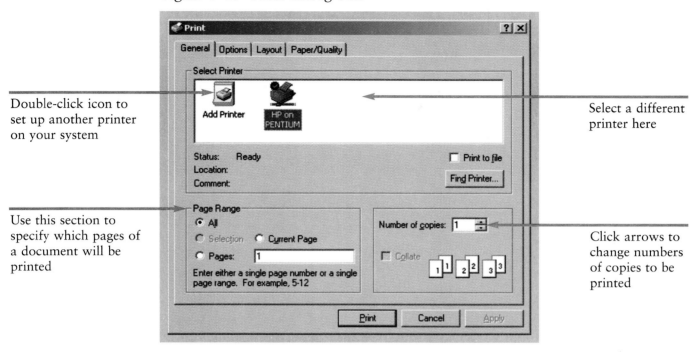

Double-click icon to
set up another printer
on your system

Select a different
printer here

Use this section to
specify which pages of
a document will be
printed

Click arrows to
change numbers
of copies to be
printed

Figure 3-14 Page Setup dialog box

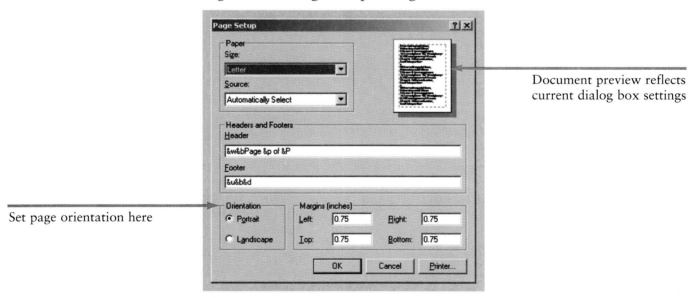

Document preview reflects
current dialog box settings

Set page orientation here

Practice

Print a copy of your browser's home page
with the Orientation set to **Landscape**.

Hot Tip

The Print dialog box's **Collate** option
allows you to print complete sets of a document in page order when you are printing
more than one copy of a multiple page
document.

Shortcuts

Function	Button/Mouse	Menu	Keyboard
Stop loading page		Click View, then click Stop	[Esc]
Refresh page		Click View, then click Refresh	[F5]
Go to browser's home page		Click View, then highlight Go To, then click Home Page	[Alt]+[Home]
Expand window to full screen view		Click View, then click Full Screen	[F11]
Access mail from IE (start Outlook Express)		Click Tools, then highlight Mail and News	[Alt], [T], [M]
Print current page		Click File, then click Print (for dialog box)	[Ctrl]+[P] (for dialog box)
Open new browser window		Click File, then highlight New, then click Window	[Ctrl]+[N]
Open new page		Click File, then click Open	[Ctrl]+[O]
Browse back	Back	Click View, then highlight Go To, then click Back	[Alt]+[Left Arrow]
Browse forward		Click View, then highlight Go To, then click Forward	[Alt]+[Right Arrow]

Identify Key Features

Name and describe the functions of the buttons indicated by callout arrows in **Figure 3-15**.

Figure 3-15 Internet Explorer's Standard Buttons toolbar

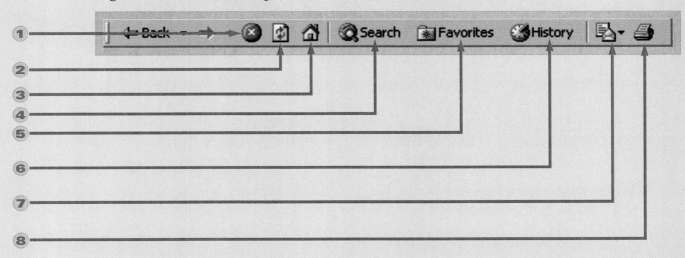

Select The Best Answer

9. Click this to go to your browser's home page

10. Dialog box that allows you to create shortcuts to pages you visit frequently

11. Language used to write Web pages

12. Protocol used to transfer data over the Web

13. Dialog box that allows you to relocate a Favorite

14. A subset of the Internet that allows users to publish documents on remote servers

15. An individual component of a Web page that can be printed independently

16. A Page Setup option

17. Reloads the current page in the browser window

18. Allows you to create buttons for your Favorites

a. Refresh button

b. World Wide Web

c. Home button

d. Links toolbar

e. Orientation

f. HTTP

g. Browse for Folder

h. HTML

i. Add Favorite dialog box

j. Frame

Quiz (continued)

Complete the Statement

19. A document's address on the Web is also known as its:

   a. EARL

   b. IRL

   c. URL

   d. HTTP

20. To help you find documents on the Web, you should use:

   a. IE's Search Explorer Bar

   b. Windows 2000's help facility

   c. Outlook Express

   d. IE's Favorites Explorer Bar

21. All of the following are popular search engines except:

   a. AltaVista

   b. MSN Search

   c. Outlook

   d. Excite

22. The Web runs on a:

   a. Linear platform

   b. Decreasing number of hosts

   c. Government-regulated network

   d. Client-server model

23. You can create a favorite for the current page by dragging and dropping the:

   a. Favorites button

   b. IE page icon

   c. Favorites Explorer Bar

   d. Current URL

24. Clicking on the Print button causes your document to be printed without:

   a. Margins

   b. Headers and Footers

   c. The appearance of the Print dialog box

   d. Frames

25. To change your browser's home page, choose the Internet Options command from the:

   a. Tools menu

   b. File menu

   c. Home page dialog box

   d. Favorites menu

26. The mouse pointer changes to a hand with a pointing finger to indicate that:

   a. The page you requested has finished loading

   b. The link you are pointing to is a Favorite

   c. You must wait until the page finishes loading

   d. You are pointing to an active link

Interactivity

Test Your Skills

1. Open Internet Explorer and practice navigating the Web:

   a. Launch Internet Explorer.

   b. If your browser is not set to open to www.msn.com, go there now.

   c. Look for a link to microsoft.com and click it to go to Microsoft's home page.

   d. Click the Privacy Policy link near the bottom of the page.

   e. Go back to Microsoft's home page.

   f. Return to the Privacy Policy page.

2. Visit a Web page whose address you have entered manually:

   a. Use the Address Bar to visit http://www.cnn.com.

   b. Stop the page before it finishes loading.

   c. Refresh the page.

3. Use the Search Explorer Bar to find Web sites about your hometown and store them as Favorites:

   a. Activate the Search Explorer Bar.

   b. Conduct a search for Web pages that relate to your hometown.

   c. Follow the links generated by the search until you have found two or three that you like.

   d. Add these sites to your Favorites list.

4. Create a new Favorites folder and move existing Favorites into it:

   a. Open the Organize Favorites dialog box.

   b. Create a new folder named [Your Hometown] Links.

   c. Move the Favorites you created in the previous step into the new folder.

   d. Rename the new folder so that its name is just that of your hometown and doesn't include the word "Links."

Interactivity (continued)

5. Print a Web page with Landscape orientation:

   a. Direct your Web browser to one of the hometown Favorites you created above.

   b. Open the Page Setup dialog box from the File menu.

   c. Change the page orientation from Portrait to Landscape, then click OK.

   d. Open the Print dialog box.

   e. Print 2 copies of the current page.

Problem Solving

1. Search the Web for information on guitars and guitar instruction. Use at least three different search engines to conduct your search. When you find helpful sites, be sure to bookmark them in appropriately named folders. Create at least four different folders to house favorites for the sites you find. Some categories you might use are: Guitar Sales, Online Instruction, and Chords and Tablature.

2. As a sales representative, you fit the title of "business traveler" perfectly. Fortunately, the World Wide Web can do wonders for your travel expenses. Various Web sites can now assist you in finding the cheapest air fares and hotel rooms available. Use the skills you have learned in this lesson to find at least three such sites on the Web. Add each site to your Favorites list. Then create a new Favorites folder named Travel Savings and move the Favorites you have added into the new folder.

3. As the Director of Human Resources at a large accounting firm, it is important for you to stay on top of the issues that affect the workforce. Chief among these is health insurance. Your approach to this topic is two-fold. You like to keep one eye on what the insurance companies are saying about themselves, and the other on what the watchdogs are saying about the insurance companies. Use your Web skills to find the Web sites of major health care providers. Store the home pages of these sites in a Favorites folder named Health Care Providers. Then focus your Web search on pages that provide reviews of, or news about, particular health care companies. Organize these pages in a Favorites folder named Health Care Reviews. Print the page that offers the best summary of current health insurance issues.

4. Your department is in the market for a new color laser printer. You have been chosen to research the purchase and recommend a printer to your boss. Use your Web skills to find out as much as you can about four top of the line color laser printers. You should search for the Web sites of companies that actually manufacture and sell the printers as well as independent reviews of printers. When you find a page on a manufacturer's site, save it as a Favorite in a folder named Printers. When you find a page that review the performance of a particular printer or printers, save it as a Favorite in a folder named Printer Reviews. After studying the four candidates you have found, select the printer that you think will best suit your department's needs (a high output rate, low maintenance, network ready, reliable service program). Create a button for the Web page of the printer you have chosen on the Links toolbar.

A

Accessories
Programs built into Windows 2000 that are useful for everyday tasks.

Active Desktop
Gives you the ability to integrate live Web content and animated pictures into your desktop.

Active window
The window you are currently using. When a window is active, its title bar changes color to differentiate it from other open windows and its program button is depressed.

Address Bar
Used for entering a Web address manually; can also be used to view a local folder or drive.

Address Book
Component of Outlook Express that allows you to store contact information.

Appearance tab
In the Display Properties dialog box, lets you customize the appearance of individual system items or apply an appearance scheme.

Attach button
Permits you to e-mail a computer file.

B

Back button
Allows you to return to the Web page or system window you viewed previously.

Background tab
In the Display Properties dialog box, used to apply wallpaper to your desktop.

Bitmap (bmp)
Basic image file format used by Windows.

Browsing
Examining Web pages in the manner of your choice.

C

CD Player
Windows application that lets you play audio CDs.

Check box
A small square box that allows you to turn a dialog box option on or off by clicking it.

Classic Style
A folder option that requires a double-click to open an icon and a single-click to select it.

Click
To press and release a mouse button in one motion; usually refers to the left mouse button.

Client-Server
A computing model in which computers known as clients request and receive data from a central computer with high storage capacity called a server.

Clipboard
A temporary storage area for cut or copied text or graphics. You can paste the contents of the Clipboard into any Windows program, such as WordPad or Microsoft Word. The Clipboard holds the information until it is replaced with another piece of text, or until the computer is shut down.

Close
To quit an application and remove its window from the desktop. The Close button appears in the upper-right corner of a window, on the title bar.

Command
Directive that carries out an application feature or provides options for carrying out a feature.

Command button
In a dialog box, a button that carries out an action. A command button usually has a label that describes its action, such as OK, Cancel, or Help. If the label is followed by an ellipsis, clicking the button displays another dialog box.

Control menu
Contains commands related to resizing, moving, and closing a window.

Control Panel
A utility used for changing computer settings. You can access the various control panels through the Start menu, My Computer, or Windows Explorer.

Copy
To place a duplicate of a file or portion thereof on the Clipboard to be pasted in another location.

Cursor
The blinking vertical line in a document window that indicates where text will appear when you type. Also referred to as the insertion point.

Cut
To remove a file, or a portion of a file, and place it on the Clipboard.

Cut and paste
To remove information from one place and insert it in another using the Clipboard as the temporary storage area.

D

Date/Time Properties dialog box
Allows you to set your system clock and calendar.

Deleted Items folder
Outlook Express folder that functions much like the Windows Recycle Bin.

Desktop
The on-screen area, created using the metaphor of a desk, that provides workspace for your computing tasks.

Dialog box
A box that explains the available command options for you to review or change before executing the command.

Disk Cleanup
Windows utility that removes unnecessary files from your computer creating more free space.

Disk Defragmenter
Windows utility that rearranges the data on your hard disk so that it can be accessed more efficiently.

Document window
The window within the application window in which a file is viewed and edited. When the document window is maximized, it shares a border and title bar with the application window.

Double-click
To press and release the mouse button twice rapidly; usually refers to the left mouse button.

Drafts folder
In Outlook Express, allows you to store messages that you have not finished composing.

Drag
To hold down the mouse button while moving the mouse.

E

Edit
To add, delete, or modify elements of a file.

E-mail
A method of sending electronic messages from one computer to another over the Internet.

Entire Network icon
Gives you access to the other workgroups that are a part of your network.

F

Favorite
A shortcut to a local, network, or Internet address that you have saved so that you can access the location easily.

Favorites Explorer Bar
Makes your Favorites menu part of the browser window so that it is always available.

Favorites menu
Allows you to store shortcuts to your favorite Web pages and other files for easy access.

File
A document that has been created and saved under a unique file name.

File hierarchy
A logical order for folders and files that resembles how you would organize files and folders in a filing cabinet. Your file hierarchy displays where your folders and files are stored on your computer.

File management
The skill of organizing files and folders.

Folders
Subdivisions of a disk that work like a filing system to help you organize files.

Folders Explorer Bar
Default left panel of Windows Explorer; shows all of the drives and folders available on your computer.

Footer
Text that appears at the bottom of a printed document.

Format
The way information appears on a page. To format means to change the appearance of data without changing its content.

Format Bar
Toolbar that allows you to format text in a WordPad document.

Formatting Toolbar
Allows you to change the characteristics of the text in an e-mail message and insert objects.

Forward button
Allows you to revisit a Web page or system window from which you have browsed back.

Forward command
Used to pass a message you have received to another e-mail address.

Frame
An independent component of a Web page.

Full
A file sharing setting that allows others to read and edit your shared files.

G

Graphical user interface (GUI)
An environment made up of meaningful symbols, icons, words, and windows that control the basic operation of a computer and the programs it runs.

H

Header
The summary information for an e-mail or newsgroup message. Also, the text that appears along the top of a printed page.

Help button
A button in a Help window that opens a dialog box or a program to provide an answer to your question.

Highlight
When an item is shaded to indicate that it has been selected.

History Explorer Bar
Displays links for all of the drives and folders or Web pages you have visited recently.

Home page

The page to which your browser opens upon launch or clicking the Home button; can also refer to the main page of a particular Web site.

Horizontal scroll bar

Changes your view laterally when all of the information in a file does not fit in the window.

Hypermedia

Text, pictures, and other objects that are linked to files on the Web and will access those files when clicked. Also known as hyperlinks.

HyperText Markup Language (HTML)

Platform-independent computer language used to write Web pages.

HyperText Transfer Protocol (HTTP)

The exchange process used by servers and clients in transferring data over the Web.

I

Icon

Pictorial representation of programs, files, and other screen elements.

Inbox

Holds the e-mail messages you have received in Outlook Express.

Inbox Assistant

Creates filters that route incoming messages to a specific folder based on criteria you supply.

Internet

A worldwide computer network made up of numerous smaller networks.

Internet Connection Wizard

Runs you through the process of setting up an Internet account.

Internet Explorer

Windows 2000's Web browsing application.

K

Keyboard shortcut

A keyboard equivalent of a menu command (e.g., [Ctrl]+[X] for Cut).

L

Landscape orientation

Page setup in which the left to right length is greater than the top to bottom length.

Launch

To start a program so you can work with it.

Links toolbar

Makes Favorites available as buttons in your browser window.

List box

A drop-down list of items. To choose an item, click the list box drop-down arrow, then click the desired item from the list.

Lurk

To read the messages on a newsgroup without participating in the discussion.

M

Map Network Drive

Command that connects your computer to a remote shared folder as if it were a local drive.

Maximize

To enlarge a window to its maximum size. Maximizing an application window causes it to fill the screen; maximizing a document window causes it to fill the application window.

Menu

A list of related commands in an application.

Menu bar

Lists the names of menus containing application commands. Click a menu name on the Menu bar to display its list of commands.

Minimize

To shrink a window to its minimum size. Minimizing an application window reduces it to a button on the Windows taskbar.

Mouse

A palm-sized, hand-operated input device that you roll on your desk to position the mouse pointer and click to select items and execute commands.

Mouse buttons

The two buttons on the mouse, called the left and right mouse buttons, that you use to make selections and issue commands.

Mouse pointer

The usually arrow-shaped cursor on the screen that you control by guiding the mouse on your desk. You use the mouse pointer to select items, drag objects, choose commands, and start or exit programs. The appearance of the mouse pointer can change depending on the task being executed.

Multitasking

The ability to run several programs on your computer at once and easily switch among them.

My Computer

A tool used to view the files and folders that are available on your computer and how they are arranged. The default icon, a PC, appears on the desktop.

My Network Places

Allows you to view and access the computers that make up your network.

Network

Two or more computers linked together to allow for the sharing and exchanging of data.

New Toolbar command

Allows you to create a custom toolbar that can be placed on the taskbar or in its own window.

Newsgroup

An electronic bulletin board on the Internet used to post messages on a specific topic.

Operating system

Controls the basic operation of your computer and the programs you run on it. Windows 2000 is an operating system.

Organize Favorites command

Allows you to rename your Favorites and restructure your Favorites hierarchy.

Outbox

Stores e-mail messages you have composed in Outlook Express until you send them.

Outlook Express

E-mail software that comes with Windows 2000.

P

Paint

Windows 2000's built-in drawing program.

Pattern

Used to fill in the area of the desktop that is not covered by wallpaper.

Personalized menus

Feature that permits the Start and Menu bar menus to adapt to your usage by temporarily hiding the commands you use infrequently so the others are more accessible.

Point

To place the mouse pointer over an item on the desktop.

Pop-up menu

The menu that appears when you right-click certain places in the Windows environment.

Portrait orientation

Traditional document setup in which the top to bottom length is greater than the left to right.

Post

To send a message to a newsgroup.

Program

A software application that performs specific tasks, such as Microsoft Word or WordPad.

Program button

The button that appears on the taskbar to indicate that an application is open. The active program is represented by an indented button.

Properties

The characteristics of a specific element (such as the mouse, keyboard, or desktop display) that you can change. Properties can also refer to characteristics of a file such as its name, type, size, and location.

R

Radio button

A small circular button in a dialog box that allows you to switch between options.

Read-Only

A file sharing setting that prevents others from editing your shared files.

Recycle Bin

An icon on the desktop that represents a temporary storage area for deleted files. Files will remain in the Recycle Bin until you empty it, at which time they are permanently removed from your computer.

Reply to All

Allows you to send a direct response to an e-mail message that is also received by each recipient of the original message.

Reply to Author

Allows you to send a direct response to an e-mail message.

Restore

To return a window to its previous size before it was resized (either maximized or minimized). A Restore button usually appears in the upper-right corner of a window, on the title bar.

Right-click

To click the right mouse button; often necessary to access specialized menus and shortcuts. (The designated right and left mouse buttons may be reversed with the Mouse control panel to accommodate user preferences.)

Run

To open an application.

S

Screen saver

A moving or changing image that covers your screen when you are not working.

ScreenTip

A yellow help box that Windows provides to explain a particular feature.

Scroll bar

A graphical device for moving vertically and horizontally through a document with the mouse. Scroll bars are located along the right and bottom edges of the document window.

Scroll bar box

A small grey box located inside a scroll bar that indicates your current position relative to the rest of the document window. You can advance a scroll bar box by dragging it, clicking the scroll bar on either side of it, or by clicking the scroll bar arrows.

Search command

Allows you to search for local or network files, other computers on your network, Internet addresses, and more.

Search engine
A Web site that generates Web links based on criteria you provide.

Search Explorer Bar
Permits you to keep an Internet search in the browser window and visit links at the same time. Also allows you to search local and network drives for files and folders.

Select
Highlighting an item to indicate that it is the active object on the screen. Usually done in order to perform some operation on the item.

Selection bar
The unmarked column on the left side of the WordPad document window that allows you to select entire lines or paragraphs of text at once.

Sent Items folder
Folder that automatically stores a copy of each e-mail message you send in Outlook Express.

Set as Wallpaper
Command that allows you to use an image as desktop wallpaper.

Shared folder
A folder that is accessible to computers other than the one it is stored on over a network.

Shortcut
A link that takes you directly to a particular file, folder, or program without having to pass through each item in its file hierarchy.

Shut down
The process you go through to turn off your computer when you finish working. After you complete this action it is safe to turn off your computer.

Sound Recorder
Windows application that lets you record and play audio.

Start button
A button on the taskbar that accesses a special menu that you use to start programs, find files, access Windows Help and more.

Stationery
A picture used to enhance the appearance of an e-mail message.

Surfing
A synonym for browsing.

System Tray
The box at the right edge of the taskbar that houses your system clock and various utility icons.

T

Task Scheduler
Allows you to automate Windows tasks.

Taskbar
A bar, usually located at the bottom of the screen, that contains the Start button, shows which programs are running by displaying their program buttons, and shows the current time.

Taskbar and Start menu command
Allows you to control the behavior and content of the taskbar and the Start menu.

Thumbnails View
Allows you to view previews of all image files in a folder rather than file icons

Title bar
The horizontal bar at the top of a window that displays the name of the document or application that appears in the window.

Toolbar
A graphical bar containing buttons that act as shortcuts for common commands.

Triple-click

In some programs, performing this action is an easy way to select an entire line or block of text.

U

Uniform Resource Locator (URL)

The address of a file on the Internet.

V

Vertical scroll bar

Moves your view up and down through a window, allowing you to view portions of a document that are not currently visible.

W

Wait box

Determines how many idle minutes Windows will wait before initializing a screen saver.

Wallpaper

A picture you apply to your desktop.

Wave (wav)

A Windows sound file.

Web

A subset of the Internet that allows users to publish documents on special computers called servers so that others (clients) can access them.

Web browser

A computer application that allows you to view documents on the World Wide Web.

Web Style

A folder option that allows you to select an icon by pointing to it and open an icon with a single click.

Web tab

In the Display Properties dialog box, used to control Active Desktop content.

Window

A rectangular area on the screen in which you view and work on files.

Windows Explorer

A tool that allows you to view the hierarchy of folders on your computer and all the subfolders and files in a selected folder. Windows Explorer is very useful for moving and copying files among folders.

Windows Media Player

Windows 2000's audio and video player, capable of playing a variety of sound and movie formats including streaming media.

WordPad

Windows 2000's built-in word processing program.

Workgroup

A group of computers that is a subdivision of a network.

Index